SEVEN LEARS

GOLGO

PLAYSCRIPT 117

SEVEN LEARS
The Pursuit of the Good

GOLGO
Sermons on Pain and Privilege

Howard Barker

JOHN CALDER · LONDON
RIVERRUN PRESS · NEW YORK

First published in Great Britain, 1990, by
John Calder (Publishers) Ltd
9–15 Neal Street, London WC2H 9TU

and in the United States of America, 1990, by
Riverrun Press Inc
1170 Broadway, New York, NY 1001

British Library Cataloguing in Publication Data
Barker, Howard *1946–*
    Seven Lears; The pursuit of the good; Golgo: Sermons on
    pain and privilege. – Playscript; 117
    I. Title
    822'.914

    ISBN 0-7145-4183-4

Library of Congress Cataloging in Publication Data has been applied for.

Typeset in 9/10 pt Times by BP Integraphics Ltd, Bath, Avon
Printed in Great Britain by Hillman Printers (Frome) Ltd, Somerset

For
Roger Frost

SEVEN LEARS
The Pursuit of the Good

INTRODUCTION

Shakespeare's *King Lear* is a family tragedy with a significant absence.

The Mother is denied existence in *King Lear*.

She is barely quoted even in the depths of rage or pity.

She was therefore expunged from memory.

This extinction can only be interpreted as repression.

She was therefore the subject of an unjust hatred.

This hatred was shared by Lear and all his daughters.

This hatred, while unjust, may have been necessary.

'The best and soundest of his time hath been
but rash ...'
Goneril, *King Lear*.

Seven Lears was first performed by The Wrestling School at the Sheffield Crucible Theatre, on 13th October, 1989 with the following cast:

LEAR	Nicholas Le Provost
CLARISSA	Jemma Redgrave
PRUDENTIA	Jane Bertish
HORBLING, SURGEON, HERDSMAN	Roger Frost
BISHOP, GONERIL	Tricia Kelly
KENT, SECOND MAN, EMPEROR, ARTHUR	Philip Franks
GLOUCESTER, OSWALD, TERRIBLE SOLDIER, FIRST MAN, LUD	Benny Young
CORDELIA, DRUMMER BOY, DUMB BEGGAR	Julie-Kate Olivier
REGAN, INVENTOR, SURGEONS ASSISTANT	Philippa Vafadari
THE CHORUS OF THE GAOLED	The Company

DESIGNED BY	Dermot Hayes
MUSIC BY	Matthew Scott
DIRECTED BY	Kenny Ireland

CHARACTERS

LEAR	A Child, later a King
LUD	His Brother
ARTHUR	His Brother
BISHOP	A Teacher
PRUDENTIA	A Widow
CLARISSA	Her Daughter, later a Queen
HORBLING	A Minister, later a Fool
KENT	A Soldier
OSWALD	A Soldier
THE TERRIBLE SOLDIER	
BOY	
THE SURGEON	
ASSISTANT	
GONERIL	A Princess
REGAN	A Princess
THE INVENTOR	
GLOUCESTER	A Vagrant, later an Earl
HERDSMAN	
CORDELIA	A Princess
THE EMPEROR OF ENDLESSLY EXPANDING TERRITORY	
FIRST MAN	Servants of the State
SECOND MAN	Servants of the State
DRUMMER	
THE GAOLED	A Chorus

FIRST LEAR

Darkness. A Pit in the Kingdom of LEAR's father. The rattle of a bunch of keys. A child's voice, full of apprehension

LUD: Let's play football! Let's fly kites!
ARTHUR: Let's build castles on the beach!
LEAR: Something bad is happening here . . .!
LUD: Something horrible!
ARTHUR: I dropped my stick!
LEAR: Something rotten, can you smell?
ARTHUR: My stick! My stick!
LUD: Horrid smell!
LEAR: Something's alive, but only just!
ARTHUR: Oh, let's build castles on the beach!
LEAR: Someone's in pain . . .!
LUD: Let's play football! Let's fly kites!
ARTHUR: I want my stick!
LEAR: That smell is pain! Be careful where you tread!
LUD: A hand! A hand! I trod on a hand!
THE GAOL: **We are the dead who aren't dead yet**
Ever so sorry
Not dead yet

The children cling together.

Whatever it did
Whatever it was
How could it justify this?
LEAR: Are you the bad, then? That you smell so badly?
ARTHUR: We are clean children and our mother loves us.
LUD: Are you our father's enemies? If so, however bad this is, it can't be bad enough for you!
THE GAOL: **We never said that we were innocent**
What's innocence?
We never claimed we had no hatred
Who has none?
We never claimed that this was arbitrary
What isn't?
LEAR: They have no light . . .!
LUD: We are the royal children, shut your mouths!
LEAR: They have no sheets . . .!

ARTHUR: **Foot-ball** ...!

LUD: Die, you horrid, stinking criminals!

ARTHUR: **Foot-ball** ...!

LEAR: Oh, you poor, wet things, I never knew the ground was full of bodies, and you've got no sheets ...!

LUD: All horrid things deserve to die ...!

ARTHUR: **Foot-ball** ...! (*He tears out,* followed by LUD. LEAR *hesitates.*)

LEAR: I shan't be king, because I am not the eldest but ... if I were king ... for one thing ... I'd stop this! (*He runs out. A ball bounces in a field. A bright sunlight fills the stage.* THE CHILDREN *wander, apart.*)

LEAR: No criticism of our father, but I wonder is it necessary that —

LUD: **Don't talk about our doings**.

LEAR: I wasn't, but I find my mind —

LUD: **Don't remind us of it, posts!**

LEAR (*taking off his shirt*): If people were good, punishment would be unnecessary, therefore —

LUD (*pointing*): **Penalty spot**.

LEAR: The function of all government must be —

LUD: We kick that way.

LEAR (*placing* ARTHUR's *shirt as second post*): The definition of, and subsequent encouragement, of goodness, surely? (LUD *prepares a flying kick off.*) Perhaps by making goodness easier, fewer people would — (LUD *boots the ball with terrific violence. It sails high and away.* LEAR *follows it with a look of incomprehension, shading his eyes.*) You've kicked it so hard it's — (LUD *puts his arm lovingly around* ARTHUR's *shoulder*) gone right over the cliff ... (*Linked together,* LUD *and* ARTHUR *walk slowly upstage.* LEAR *sits on the ground to wait.*) You would define goodness in such a way that ordinary people — who at the moment are so horribly attracted to bad things and immoral actions — would find it simple to appreciate and consequently act upon — (*He stops. He is inspired.*) No! No! That's wrong! The opposite is the case! That's it! You make goodness difficult, if anything. You make it apparently impossible to achieve! It then becomes compelling, it becomes a victory, rather as acts of badness seem a triumph now! What you need to do — (*He turns. His brothers have stopped at the very edge of the cliff and look down. Pause.*) I think, Lud, when you are king, the correct approach to punishment would be — (*They fall out of sight, together. Pause.* LEAR *stares, fixedly. A thin wind blows. He utters a cry, terrible and deep. At last, a* BISHOP *enters.*)

BISHOP: I am your education.

LEAR: I am hard to educate because I was born wise.

BISHOP: That's something everybody knows.

LEAR: I will be relentlessly critical and nothing you say will I take on trust. Why should I?

BISHOP: Why should you, after all?

LEAR: This is not arrogance on my part.

BISHOP: No, indeed.

LEAR: On the basis of mutual study we may answer some questions that have haunted me since birth.

BISHOP: My imagination is at your disposal.

LEAR: I must warn you I am peevish at times and come out in rashes, I suppose you know that.

BISHOP: I know everything about you.

LEAR: Everything? No one can know everything.

BISHOP: I know your brothers killed themselves. I know you think of death yourself. I know you cry for animals but harbour hatreds you yourself do not yet understand.

LEAR: Yes. How will you educate me?

BISHOP: I will educate you by showing you how bad I am. Because I am a bad man you will learn much from me. I will tell you nothing but what accords with my experience, which is not a happy one. Hope, for example, I have dispensed with entirely. There will be no books because you know the books and have digested them. I detest all untruths, but especially those which are sentimental, and I will beat you sometimes, for which I have authority. Almost certainly, these beatings will appear to you unjustified. I will explode in rages and then fawn on you. I may kiss your body and then ignore you for days on end. You will detest me and your innate sense of justice will cry out for satisfaction. When one day, that cry ceases, your education will be over. God alone know why your father appointed me.

SECOND LEAR

The CHORUS *are disposed about the stage.* LEAR, *a youth, comes among them as if between trees. He drops to his knees. He shudders. He laughs. He clasps his head.*

LEAR: I'm in such
    I'm in such
    I won't say ecstasy
    I won't say

He shudders with emotion. A WOMAN *enters. She extends a hand to him.*

Don't touch! (*He rests his forehead on the ground.*)

PRUDENTIA: Oh, you bastard, you mistreat me, and I a woman of distinction. Oh, you shallow and temperamental manipulator of emotion, do you think I can't see through you? And your love is rough. Your love is **rough**.

LEAR: Yes. Go back to your books now. You are a lawyer, aren't you? Study the laws of infatuation.

PRUDENTIA: Our next meeting, will it —

LEAR: Next?

PRUDENTIA: Meeting, yes, will it be —

LEAR: **Next meeting? No sooner has she. No sooner have we than. What other meetings**? (*She looks at him.*) Memorize me. Store my touch. (*She turns to go.*) **She wants a meeting**! (*She starts to walk away.*) Please come back! (*She stops.*) I am so thin, and boastful, and poor-minded, I am so empty and shallow as a tin bowl, ping! Love my emptiness, and don't run to men of quality and honesty, I will execute all men of character if you do, all those of deep soul who command the loyalty of women, the bearded and the bald, the calm-eyed and the knowing, love your tin bowl or it's a massacre. Ping! (*He extends a hand. She goes to put it to her lips.*) Not there. (*She places it on her belly.*)

CLARISSA (*Off*): Mother . . .!

A girl enters.

CLARISSA: Mother . . .! (PRUDENTIA *turns to face her daughter.*) You are everywhere these days except where you should be! That sounds silly but. And you smell strangely. Now look at you! This was the last place I expected to. But now I think, where is the last place she might be, go there! And that is always where I find you! (*She laughs.*) And you smell strangely . . . This is such a miserable corner. No sun! Your law books are quite dusty. What is attractive about these sunless corners? And you smell strangely.

LEAR: I am a tin bowl. Ping!

PRUDENTIA: Do you know, there is a law in life —

LEAR: A law in life!

PRUDENTIA: Which says, she who habitually absents herself is best left undiscovered?

LEAR: Ping! Remember the law! Ping!

CLARISSA: Why does he say that so often?

PRUDENTIA: I smell oddly because I have been in Heaven.

LEAR (*standing*): I met a poet, and he said —

PRUDENTIA: Heaven clings.

LEAR: Very gravely, very portentously —

PRUDENTIA: It stains.

LEAR: His eyes on mine, how I detested him, how I hate the gravity of poets. '**Great love lasts through winters.**' (*Pause. He pulls a face of contempt.*) I, of course, shrank at the wisdom. I, being a tin bowl, shallowly vibrated at his profound bass notes. I tinkled on the table. Do you not feel oppressed by the wise, their laws and their shuddering complacency, the fact is I am girl-mad, which is shallowness itself, and most becoming in a tin bowl! Ping! (*He looks at CLARISSA. Pause.*)

CLARISSA: You are funny, for a prince. I think you can't command yet, much respect, can he? But here is my mother with him! So there is respect, of some kind, obviously. (*She turns to her mother.*) I came to tell you what no longer seems significant.

PRUDENTIA: Why? Tell me.

CLARISSA: I can't. It no longer seems — it has no —

PRUDENTIA: But all the same.

CLARISSA: I would feel humiliated, since it so obviously lacks significance. What delighted me for half an hour suddenly seems pitiful. I suppose because you have been in Heaven and I only thought I was ... **I don't see why heaven needs to stink**. (*Pause*) My bird is found. (*Pause*)

PRUDENTIA: Bird ... (*Pause*)

CLARISSA: You don't remember my bird.

PRUDENTIA: Yes, I —

CLARISSA: No, you have entirely —

PRUDENTIA: No, I don't think I —

CLARISSA: You have entirely obliterated my bird from your memory, and why shouldn't you? (*Pause*)

PRUDENTIA: Yes. I had. I'm sorry, Clarissa, yes.

CLARISSA: Yes. I am not you, and you are not me, it is futile we rehearse an intimacy which no longer exists, I am not critical, you understand, I only —

PRUDENTIA: Clarissa —

CLARISSA: I only want to be honest. (*Pause*) From this moment I mark the closure of my childhood. I am sixteen, this is farewell and a dismal corner is correct for it. Shake hands. (*She puts out a hand.*)

PRUDENTIA: Of course not.

CLARISSA: Very well. Thank you for your love. I am most grateful.

LEAR: Ping! I remember your bird very well!

CLARISSA: Why does everybody lie?

LEAR: I don't lie, I exaggerate.

CLARISSA: You think you are amusing, but you are an exhibitionist.

LEAR: I think I am the most melancholy and degenerate character, so sunk in contemplation of myself I walk with stooping shoulders and lids half-draped over my never-sparkling eyes, white-skinned with horror of the sunshine and prematurely bald, incapable of friendship and though wealthy, inclined to theft. I steal the clothes of women and insinuate myself in wardrobes listening to their acts of love. Poverty disgusts me, but equally does wealth. I listen to old men, at least for seven sentences and go early to bed, but your bird has red feathers and was brought from China.

CLARISSA: Yes. But I am looking for friend now, not an idiot. (*She turns to go.*)

LEAR: If you fuck with a greybeard, I'll — If you go down on quiet streets and bed with a musician, I'll — (*He kicks a stone.* PRUDENTIA *goes out with* CLARISSA.)

THE GAOL: **We are the dead**

> **We are the cruel**
> **We no longer need**
> **To mouth fidelities**

FIRST VOICE: **I am the torturer**

SECOND VOICE: **I am the victim**

BOTH: **What brought us into such proximity?**

THIRD VOICE: **I am the philosopher**

FOURTH VOICE: **I am the peasant**

BOTH: **What brought us into such unhealthy intimacy?** (*A peal of laughter. They depart.*)

LEAR: How proud I was, when she did not resist my hand. How its smooth gliding to her heat was uncontested. **Youth — its piquancy!** How she forgives me everything. How she is tolerant of my dog's paws in her liquidity. **Youth – its intransigence!** She loves me not for what I am but for what I will be. To what I will be she believes herself a **significant contributor**. Oh, the vanity! And she complains if I turn her too swiftly on her face. Ow, she says. Some arthritic. Some rheumatic. Ow! (*He covers his face with his hands.*) I must recover. I must shed. I must emerge from this — cruelty ...! (*The* BISHOP *enters.* LEAR *hurries to him.*) I have seen a girl I want! (*The* BISHOP *puts his arm around* LEAR.) Of course this may be a passing feeling. It may be slight. It may be trivial. Her hair is gold and her mouth far from luscious but. And gold is not a colour I much care for. It is tangled. Naturally, it's tangled. **Not her hair the emotion**. I don't think anything should stand in the way of my desire, do you? On the other hand, what good can come from it? I think what I want I should have. To be deprived, what good is it? And pain, yes, obviously pain will be experienced, but it is tangled. I am fucking with the mother. (*Pause*)

BISHOP: Have the mother murdered.

LEAR: I considered that! The moment I saw the daughter I considered that. The thought leapt to the very forefront of my mind, it knocked against my skull demanding my attention, one look and I thought, the mother has to die! (*Pause*) But no, I love the mother.

BISHOP: Abduct the daughter.

LEAR: Abduct her, yes! Would you help with that? No, it's not what I want ...

BISHOP: You change, my son.

LEAR: I do! I do change! Hourly! The surface of my mind is like the boiling tar vat, God knows what may bubble from the bottom, tar in the eye! (*Pause*) I think I must adore this child Clarissa. I think this is religion. What else is it? Do you recognize religion? My considerateness, my solicitude — what else is it?

BISHOP: I want to show you cruelty.

LEAR: Yes.

BISHOP: I want to teach you indifference.

LEAR: Yes.

BISHOP: Because you are in danger.

LEAR: Am I? Yes, I am.

BISHOP: From your own brilliance.

LEAR: Yes! (*A lamp is lowered on a chain, a cold wind.*) Hold my hand!

THE GAOL *murmers*.

BISHOP: Look, the gaol is full! Which is excellent!

LEAR: Excellent? Why excellent?

BISHOP: If some are to be free, others must be unfree, or they could not know freedom.

THE GAOL: **Don't turn off the light**
We long for the light
How else can we lodge in your memory?

LEAR: Are they guilty or innocent?

BISHOP: They are all guilty of something, even if it is not the cause of their punishment.

LEAR: But so are we all!

BISHOP: That's perfectly true, but it alters nothing.

THE GAOL: **Lear!**
Ten years since your last intrusion and you are
Now a bigger prince!

LEAR: Yes, and how ugly you are ! I may have changed but you have not . . . my brother could not bear your ugliness . . .!

BISHOP: The suffering are the least objective, they are swamped in sentiment as they are by sewage. They think, if only others knew our pain, they would cry out, end it! But not so! First error of the conscience-ridden!

LEAR: But isn't this injustice?

THE GAOL: **Injustice yes**
That is the word for it
Remember the word when you go back into the light
Inscribe it on your life

BISHOP: We can go to dinner now. We eat. We drink. We lie on clean mattresses.

LEAR: No, no, that is unthinkable!

BISHOP: Think it! You must think it! (*He seizes* LEAR.) Boy, you must think and swallow it!

LEAR: **Can't eat**!

BISHOP: Must hold these in your head and still pick up the crystal glasses!

THE GAOL: **Lear**
Soon
Lear
Soon
The King dies

BISHOP: You see, their inextinguishable optimism!

LEAR: I'll act! I'll act, I promise!

BISHOP (*drawing* LEAR *into an embrace*): I am trustworthy.

LEAR (*trying to escape him*): Yes —

BISHOP: I am utterly and wholly trustworthy.

LEAR: All right —

BISHOP: And I love you.

LEAR: Yes —

BISHOP: No one more.

LEAR: Yes, yes! My loved one. My true father. But all you say I can't take heed of. And one day, possibly I'll kill you. Loving you just the same. Loving you undiminished.

BISHOP (*freeing him from his arms*): Yes. (*The lamp is drawn away.*) What's a life? (*He goes out*).

What's a life . . .! (LEAR *is alone on stage. He sits*).

LEAR: The poor are not the same as the rich. The poor have got no money! (*He claps his hands.*)

That's an untruth! The truth is, they are not the same as the rich. Having no money, they became different. (TWO FIGURES *enter, equipped.*)

The innocent are the same as the guilty! They were merely looking the other way! (*He claps his hands.*)

Untrue! Another untruth! The innocent exerted themselves to be inno-cent. Difficult. Difficult. (THE FIGURES *cross the stage, he calls to them*)

Is there a war on? (*He gets up and scuttles to them.*)

I know nothing! I'm told nothing! On the other hand, I don't enquire. (*They gawp at him.*)

Take me. It's unnecessary I know the details, the causes and so on. And stabbing you can teach me on the way. Do you know who I am?

SOLDIERS: Prince Lear.

LEAR: Me, yes. Soon to be. Imminently, your master. What war is this? My father takes a long time dying. Are you making for the frontiers? **Defend them with your life**. No, run away if you want to. I permit it. There. Permission. (*He slaps their hands with his own.*)

Fleeing licence (*He laughs.*)

I talk gibberish because I'm not the monarch. Come monarchy, all statements I recant. All oaths, in the bin. (*They turn to go.*)

He's dying, but so slowly. So laboured his departure it is miserable to watch. **Don't go**. (*They stop.*)

I know what you're thinking. You are thinking — fuck this for an heir apparent. (*They laugh, frankly. So does* LEAR. HORBLING, *a minister, enters.*)

HORBLING: Your father is sinking.

LEAR: Sinking? Still? How farther can he sink?

HORBLING: I inform you. I inform you, merely. (*He turns to go.*)

LEAR: **I think you should enjoy me**. (HORBLING *stops.*)

I think you should luxuriate in my infantilism, which undoubtedly must have its rim, the comic preface to unmitigated cruelty. **The heads**

will make a pyramid to the stars. (HORBLING *goes out*. THE SOLDIERS *prepare to march*.)

Listen, I am barmy for a skinny girl and infatuated with her mother — (*They bow and march off*.)

Yes. I respect that. Yes.

I wish I had a brother! (FIGURES *appear, carrying a body on a bier.* LEAR *turns his back on it, shrinks*.)

LEAR: Listen, I am playing tennis! Don't attempt to dissuade me because youth needs exercise, it must be flexed about the muscles and I have sat about so long **don't bring him in I can't** — (*They progress. They put down the bier. Pause*.)

My sense is I shall not do this job well. Is that your sense? (*He climbs to his feet, and goes towards the body with a resolute movement. Suddenly he stops and points*.)

LEAR: Red bird! (*He follows it with his eyes.* CLARISSA *enters, with a cage in her hand*.)

CLARISSA: Gone again . . .!

LEAR: The first thing is I go to bed early. Please make a note of that, and second — (*He stops, rushes to his father's body and seizes it in his arms, rocking it to and fro and moaning. Pause*. CLARISSA *puts the cage on the floor and walks to him*.)

CLARISSA: You should not do that. Whatever the feeling. You should not do that because in governors extremes of emotion are not liked. (*He continues to sob*.) And anyway, I think you are pretending. (*She sees the bird*.) There it goes! (*She follows it off*.) (*Pause* LEAR *releases his father's body*.)

LEAR: Bury him. I shan't attend (*He walks away. The carry the bier*. HORBLING *attends on* LEAR, *patiently*.)

HORBLING: I was your father's minister.

LEAR: I know the face.

HORBLING: And gave ten years of good advice.

LEAR: Excellent. And yet he died.

HORBLING: On finance, planning, and on policy towards the rival states.

LEAR: We still exist, so excellent.

HORBLING: I had particular regard to harvests, which in all my years were poor, and yet there was no famine.

LEAR: I think —

HORBLING: And land reform was something of a speciality. The draining of the marsh beyond the river yielded fifty thousand acres. Here I propose a settlement for landless peasants.

LEAR: I think —

HORBLING: You ask me how this can be managed? Treaties of friendship with the Irish and the Cornish will reduce the need for soldiers, which will release the necessary labour and save the expense of weapons. Furthermore —

LEAR: I think —

HORBLING: I have prepared in detail plans for the ten years hence which I should like to show you, but in the meantime, this is the summary. (*He extends a sheaf of papers, crisp.* LEAR *looks at him, without taking the papers.*)

LEAR: You are so good at things. Obviously, so good at things. And yet I have no fool. (*Pause*)

HORBLING: Fool?

LEAR: Have I? Lando is senile. Whoever laughs at Lando now?

HORBLING: Well, this is not my field of expertise but Lando could be pensioned and the post advertised, of course.

LEAR: Lando did nothing but make ridicule of women. Their fat arses and so on. So they have fat arses.

HORBLING: Yes . . . I was never greatly amused by Lando . . .

LEAR: You do it. (*Pause*)

HORBLING: Do —

LEAR: Why not? Bring to it the same invention as you bring to drainage or economy. And give those to your successor. (HORBLING's *face is aghast.*) Oh, but this is promotion! (HORBLING *is unconsoled.*) And this way, I will have your best, surely? You will, in this function, be unconstrained by duty, conscience, or whatever drives you to make such squiggles on the paper . . .

HORBLING: **My skills are all in government!**

LEAR: No, that's false modesty and impossible to credit . . . (HOR-BLING *looks at the floor, then bows and starts to withdraw.*) Careful . . .! And be funny . . .! (*He goes out, passing* PRUDENTIA, *who, alone with him, opens her arms. He runs to her.*)

LEAR: Men hate me!

PRUDENTIA: No, no . . .

LEAR: Hate me, yes!

PRUDENTIA: No, but bury your father —

LEAR: No!

PRUDENTIA: Think of the people, the people will deduce —

LEAR: **I decline, I decline, and all deductions, pox!** Listen, I think I am alive for one reason, and that is you. But listen again. The you must be as I create her. The you gives no advice. That comes by volume from old men and clerks. Kiss me. Oh, hot and thick skirts, hide me, woollens, linens, silks, hide me, the odour of deep cloths and waterfalls of shift, do you have a centre, hide a mad child there!

PRUDENTIA: My genius. My rare thing. Do not die.

LEAR: Shan't die . . .

PRUDENTIA: My magician, my liar, don't be murdered . . .

LEAR: Shan't be.

PRUDENTIA: Promise!

LEAR: Can't. Nothing will I promise, and never anything on oath. (*He detaches himself.*) Why call me a liar?

PRUDENTIA : Did I? I must long to be lied to. (*Pause*)

LEAR: Yes . . . That also might be a sign of love . . . go now . . . (*She goes to leave.*) I must fuck your daughter. (*She stops.*) I must. *Pause*) And someone will. It must be better it were me.

PRUDENTIA: That would so injure me.

LEAR: I'd best not tell you, then. (*Pause.* PRUDENTIA *grapples with the idea.* LEAR *watches her.*)

PRUDENTIA: This feeling . . . your feeling for . . . my daughter . . . can be explained . . . can only be explained by . . . my daughter being . . .

LEAR: Your daughter, yes. I dare say. (*Pause*)

PRUDENTIA: So in one respect at least . . . it's . . . profoundly tied to me . . . and yet another manifestation . . . of our intimacy . . . couldn't that be said . . .?

LEAR: It could be said.

PRUDENTIA: It could be, yes. I see your point.

LEAR: My point? But you made it. (*She goes out, thoughtfully. He watches her.*) Oh, kindness . . .! Oh, decency . . .!

THE GAOL: **Lear**
  Can we address you
  Lear
  The testament of torturers and victims
  Our strange collaboration
  The first and terrible discovery
  When one lie fails
  We are irresistibly attracted to its opposite

LEAR: I was born ancient, and I must discover infancy. I was worn wise, and I must find ignorance. Or I will suffer . . . (CLARISSA *enters, pristine.*)

CLARISSA: I think you want me to admire you. In many ways I doubt it would be no compliment if I praised things merely to please you. That would not be friendship, would it? Don't you agree? So I will say — as best I can — only the truth. You will say, of course, what's truth, you do that all the time, but where does that get us? Not very far, I think. (*Pause. He smiles at her.*) I am glad to be invited to your house, but also wonder why. I am not very fascinating. I am sixteen. How can I be fascinating? (*Pause.* LEAR *goes uneasily towards her.*)

LEAR: Well . . . it's . . . well . . . I . . . well, now you . . . (*He smiles, stops.*) Speechless! (*He throws up his hands.* SERVANTS *appear, carrying a lavish table.*)
  Do sit!
  And feel —
  The absolute and uncommon pleasure of knowing nothing secret exists between us!

CLARISSA (*accepting a chair*): I do feel that.

LEAR: You do? Excellent! (*Pause. He taps his fingers. Food is transported to the table.*) Commonly I find, alone with a woman, so much unsaid. Much speaking but so much unarticulated. Now, with you —

CLARISSA: I say whatever comes into my head!

LEAR: Excellent! This is an Irish fruit. Don't you feel a long way from me? Not a very sweet fruit but should all fruit be sweet? I don't see why. I can hardly see you! (*The* SERVANTS *are active.*) Don't you love table-cloths? This one is Dutch and took the woman eighty weeks to manufacture. Am I boring you? When my father died he left three tons of linen. I do not exaggerate. Give her some wine.

CLARISSA: No alcohol!

LEAR: Of course no alcohol. This is a Scottish thing, no grape has been within a mile of it. Why no alcohol, it is not prohibited.

CLARISSA: I like to be myself.

LEAR: Well, she is the one I invited. Isn't this pleasant, and you are excellent company.

CLARISSA: That can't be true.

LEAR: It is true.

CLARISSA: It can't be true, I've said nothing and now I feel foolish. Please don't lie even for kindness. Where is the virtue in it?

LEAR: Do you like this room? It was decorated by Persian gardeners. (*She laughs.*) It was! (*He smiles at her.*) It was! I love to see you laugh. I love your teeth, which are not even, but who likes even teeth? My father brought them here to plant the oriental garden but — (*She suddenly stands, terrifyingly.*)

CLARISSA: **This is fatuous**. (*Pause*)

LEAR: They were surplus to requirements . . . (*She glares at him.*)

CLARISSA: You do not want to lunch with me.

LEAR: No.

CLARISSA: It's something else you want and this is just —

LEAR: Yes. And conversation is a screen. A futile screen in your case, since you are so —

CLARISSA: You are going to flatter me and I hate —

LEAR: I was! I was! All part of my conspiracy to —

CLARISSA: **If you love me say so**. (*Pause*) Or. (*Pause*) What do you want to do with me? Undress me? (*Pause*) I find this difficult but however difficult it is vastly preferable to lies, fruitcake, tablecloths and so on. What do you want to do? Handle me down below? There, I said I would respect you more if you simply told me what it is you want. Now I'm blushing but that is preferable to. Oh, I'm vilely uncomfortable and I have homework to do! (GONERIL *and* REGAN *enter.*)

GONERIL/REGAN: We are the children of the union! Oh, father. Oh, mother, spare us the sights and sounds of struggle! (*Pause.* LEAR *gets up.*)

LEAR: I want to see you naked.

GONERIL/REGAN: Oh, father, this is the spectacle that brought you daughters! Do you not know even a look has consequences?

CLARISSA: I think that is probably the first honest thing you've said to me! I think we can be friends if you are honest. It isn't difficult, is it? Honesty? (*He looks at her.*) But of course you can't see me because —

GONERIL/REGAN: Only a look!

CLARISSA: A look would only —

GONERIL/REGAN: Give him a look!

CLARISSA: And that would hardly be the end of it so —

GONERIL/REGAN: We want to be born! We want to be born! (*Pause*)

LEAR: I must see you and the door is locked.

GONERIL/REGAN: **We are going to be born! We are going to be born! insist on it!** (*Pause*)

CLARISSA: Is that expression meant to frighten me? It really is a rather silly face and — (*He slaps her. She shudders, and then masters herself.*) I want to go home now.

LEAR: Impossible.

CLARISSA: I said.

LEAR: And I denied.

CLARISSA: **Then you are an idiot.** (*She glares at him.*) Nakedness can be so cold. Can be so granite. Do you want granite? Here's granite! (*She drags up her dress violently. Her belly is revealed. Her manner humiliates him.*) You foolish man. What use is it? Unless I feel? Unless I want? Dead iron on a mountain. (*She drops her dress.*) Give me the key now, Lear. (*He shrugs.*)

LEAR: Not locked. (*She starts to go out.*)

LEAR: We must be married. (*She stops.*) It's obvious to me. The pain and. The grinding and. The punishment. Clarissa. (*A wind.*)

THIRD LEAR

A battlefield following a defeat. Figures drift over the stage. HORBLING, *in a filthy greatcoat, shaking a bellstick.*

HORBLING: Humour.

LEAR (*offstage*): Kill the prisoners!

HORBLING (*sitting*): Humour is the grating of impertinence upon catastrophe.

LEAR (*entering, supported by* KENT *and* OSWALD): Burn the villages!

HORBLING: Am I academic? I was made that way.

LEAR: And all the infants, massacre!

HORBLING: I bring to foolishness the erudition of a scholar, which is an obstacle, I admit.

LEAR (*as they help him onto a tarpaulin*): Hang all the citizens! Are the prisoners dead yet?

KENT: There were no prisoners, sire.

HORBLING: But he is tolerant. I have yet to make him laugh.

LEAR: I love to kill! Throat high in killing!

KENT (*to others off*): Brandy, over here!

LEAR: Who panicked, then? Who fled?

OSWALD: We did.

LEAR: No, surely, we haven't passed this way before?

OSWALD: We fled wrongly.

KENT: The army fled in one direction, and we fled in the other. They fled home, and we —

OSWALD: Deeper still into the enemy's territory.

FOOL: Humour! Humour is the consolation of impotence! Am I academic? I don't intend to be. (*A* SOLDIER *enters with a brandy flask. They nourish* LEAR.)

KENT: Four thousand miles, if we can make it.

LEAR: Put the lights out! Don't tread on twigs! And make yourselves earth colour. Be clay! This is only the first of my many victories.

OSWALD: We have been warned . . .

LEAR: Pity the dead, though . . . pity the common and the uncommon also . . . there was a singer in the bodyguard who —

OSWALD: Dead —

LEAR: Call him anyway!

OSWALD: Jack! (*Pause*) No Jack.

LEAR: Extinguish all lamps! Is no one listening?

KENT: They are the lamps of the enemy, they are seeking us to kill.

LEAR: Understandable, we have burned their country. But let me talk to them. I don't see grounds for malice.

OSWALD: We have spoiled their peace and happiness!

LEAR: Admittedly, but someone would have done so. So many buildings, such fertile crops. Jealousy alone ensured someone would have put them to the torch. Let me talk to them.

KENT: I shan't stop you.

LEAR (*staggering to his feet*): I'll say Lear's army was no more than fate, no more than hurricane.

KENT: Yes, try saying that.

LEAR: And therefore temper is as appropriate as bawling at the weather, and vengeance as absurd as stabbing wind.

KENT: Do try that argument.

LEAR: As for the dead, they would have died in any case, complaining, sick and senile, which is a burden on the state.

OSWALD (*pointing*): They're over there . . . (*He points to small lights moving.* LEAR *pulls his greatcoat round him, begins to move off.*)

HORBLING: Majesty! (*He looks back.*) Stay with me.

LEAR: They'll miss us if we don't accost them. They'll pass us by.

HORBLING: Stay, and write your wisdom in a letter. You see I think its truth will numb them, as if, when standing too close to a bell, its boom is staggering, and then they might misuse you. But from a distance, in the quiet of contemplation, the bell is music. Write it in a letter, and then your truth might have a chance. (*Pause*)

LEAR: Yes. That's good. (*Suddenly he lets out a terrible cry, and covering his face with his hands, shudders with the horror.* HORBLING *embraces him, rocks with him.*) I saw so many corpses!

HORBLING: Yes.

LEAR: I saw so many eyes!

HORBLING: Yes.

LEAR: Eyes hopped! Eyes wriggled! **Bang!** And out came eyes!

HORBLING: They do ...

LEAR: Clang goes the club!

HORBLING: Out come the eyes ... (*Pause. They wait for* LEAR *to recover. He adjusts himself. He looks around him.*)

LEAR: Thank you for your patience. It's obvious I am not yet in all departments fit to govern. (*They look at the floor.*)

I say, demonstrably, I am not, and this disaster is the proof. (*Pause*)

I say you would be well within your rights to put your daggers to my throat and end it. All of you. Now. Not legitimate, but right. (*Pause*)

Rush me if you will and quickly, I shan't lift a finger. (*Pause*)

Leave me tongue-stiff in the dark, who'd stoop to call it murder, I wish I had a brother. (*Pause*)

His body lay in Asia, what a clown ... (*He indulges.*)

Stabbed by his lieutenants in the Caucasus, this monarch little known ... (*He watches.*)

But. (*Pause*)

Lear now has this thing in his heart which no successor owns. A treasure. An ingot, hard beneath the bone. (*He looks from one to the other.*)

Error.

Oh, the heat of error, and its light ... come, warm yourself at error, who else has this? All this dead, and all these eyes, are waste if I'm not used for further government. I'm grown. (*He shrugs.*)

Of course, this argument is difficult, when you're knee-deep in clot and vein. (HORBLING *breaks the silence with a compulsive shaking of his bells, a bitter, fury of ringing. He stops.*)

KENT: Lear is shit. Lear is vomit.

LEAR: Yes.

KENT: Oh, my dead loves out there!

LEAR: Yes.

KENT: Oh, my better-than-any-woman things, my lovelier-than-cunt brigades, all flat, all pulp!

LEAR: Yes. (*He stares at* LEAR, *but does not move.* HORBLING *in a paroxysm, shakes the bells again.*)

OSWALD: I should kill you now, and scraping home in rags from fifteen months of vagrancy, say honour me, for I struck down the thing that piped us into swamping death, **you chose that ground**.

LEAR: Yes.

      But that was another Lear.

      Already I don't know him. He also lies among the reeds. (OSWALD *wavers.* HORBLING *exclaims.*)

HORBLING: Stab him now! I have the policies! I have the plans of reconstruction! Stab him now! New currency! New industry, clothes for the starving, dinner for the naked. Stab him, then! I predict a marginal increase in taxes, but silent buses, I've got the documents, why don't you stab! (*He tears off his cap and holds out the plans.* KENT *stares.*)

OSWALD (*Lying flat*): Lights ...! (*They all duck, but for* LEAR, *who climbs to his feet. Pause. Lights flicker.*)

LEAR: Death will either occur, or if not, I shall be better for having been exposed to it. In any event, it can't be meaningless ... (*He walks offstage towards the lights which bob, and then are stationary. Pause.*)
Clar-issa! (*A cheer from offstage.* CLARISSA *enters with new troops.* LEAR *draped about her.* HORBLING *immediately begins hopping about ringing the bells febrilely as if to demonstrate his innocuous character.*)

LEAR: She!
She!
God's own is there is a God!
Perfection if perfection is!

KENT (*kneeling*): Oh, Christ in ecstasy, how did this come about?

CLARISSA: We are the Second Army.

OSWALD: Second?

CLARISSA: Who came here by a different route, and found a swamp of corpses, all our colour. Through these we searched for Lear.

LEAR: I was not dead!

CLARISSA: This army will cover your withdrawal.

LEAR: Withdrawal? But we have new troops!

KENT: Withdrawal, yes.

LEAR: **Who says withdrawal! Who!** (KENT *is silent.*)

CLARISSA: The enemy is also tired, and will let us out the country, which this time we should not burn, but tread with exaggerated care, like men who were once drunk, but in the morning rather shame-faced, replace the broken fence posts in the gardens. (*Pause.* LEAR *looks at her, conceding.*)

KENT (*rising*): We'll wash, if you've the patience, and when you say so, march. (*He and* OSWALD *go out.*)

LEAR: Kent likes me. He says I have kind eyes. And when I said destroy me, he hung back ...

HORBLING: And me! I said things so ridiculous it made execution improbable. Improbable! What more can you hope for! (*He smiles, weakly.* LEAR *falls into* CLARISSA's *arms.*)

LEAR: Hold me ...! I'm real ...! I do exist, don't I? Hold me ...! (THE GAOL *appear to* LEAR.) I've not forgotten you ...! I have you very much in mind ...!
I want my name on a column
I want my name on a scroll
Time to unlock the gaol! Or maybe not!

CLARISSA: Ssh ... I came for you ...

LEAR: It is not the circumstance, it is the exposure, it is not the subject but the experience which —

CLARISSA: Shh ... I'm here ...

LEAR: I mean —

CLARISSA: Shh —

LEAR (*feverish*): Oh, let me think — oh, let me — disaster was not the failure — but the purpose of the war! (*He stares at her. She wipes his face.*)

HORBLING: It's hard to be a fool with this monarch. I meet many fools now and they say, the job is not what it was. What was it, then, I say, I am not a trained fool, I am a novice. They tell me you could do well at one time saying out loud the first thing that came in your head. Any shit. Any trivia. This was called Fool's Wisdom. But now ... you see ... there's no future in that one. (*He looks to* CLARISSA.) Take me home, Miss, I have a longing to sit in a garden ... (*He goes out.* LEAR *looks at* CLARISSA.)

LEAR: You are going to criticize me ...

CLARISSA: Who else will, if I don't ... (*He shakes his head.*) I must, Lear ... (*He nods.*)

I must because to swallow criticism in the interests of false harmony would be —

LEAR: False? (*Pause*)

CLARISSA: It is my nature and impossible to —

LEAR: Oh, look, your knee! Through all the filth of campaign, **knee**! I was ready to die — no — more than ready, yearning to die — and that knee reminds me — **the momentous loss**. (*He extends his hand slowly.*) I dare not touch it. How I want to but I won't. I'll torture my already flogged imagination. **Fingers wait**! (*He slaps his hand with the other.*) I won't say I've missed your sex exactly. It was stiff and — it was board on sand if I remember, us — a strange collision, grit not fluid, glass not dew, but I thought again and again, I want what we can not, I want what we do not, the possibility of you, more than the plunging pleasures I have on occasions — needless to relate — indulged elsewhere. Let me touch. (*He kisses her knee.*)

CLARISSA: You must be sensible, and hear advice. (*He kisses it again, kneeling.*) You must regard the judgement of others as equal to your own. I think if this is to be a happy kingdom you must study good, which is not difficult, and do it. I will help you. I will criticise you, and I will say when you are childish or petulant, and you must try to overcome the flaws in what is otherwise, I am sure, a decent character! (*Pause. He stares at the knee.*) You are often amusing, which is surely a sign of goodness! (*He does not meet her eyes.*)

LEAR: How far I've come. They say three thousand miles of marching, and the villages all roofless where we trod. I am no longer what I was. But you, equally travelled, are more yourself than ever.

CLARISSA: What was good in me, through seeing, is now more good. What was less good, there is less of.

LEAR: **What is this good**? (*He sways, seized, pained. She looks at him. He uncurls, like screwed paper. Pause.*) And is your mother —

CLARISSA: Yes. She's well ... (*He stands.*)

LEAR: Clarissa, if I am a child, it is because a child must know. Its ravings are the protests of the uninstructed. It thinks the sky is a false barrier, and the floor, pretence. It raves less, year by year, as all the barriers are demonstrated to be real, and insurmountable. I am still in my pen, and so I squeal. But thank you. And now I must see you undressed, look at your taut belly and think, childlike, it must be a fruit and a squirming animal, both.

Darkness. A drum taps. In the light of morning SOLDIERS *and* FOL-
LOWERS *assemble in a ragged line, shouldering their packs.* CLARISSA
enters, overcoated, a general. She walks among them, making her address.

CLARISSA: I am a queen, and you are peasants. There is the first thing. I am not like you, and cannot call you brothers. So you know me as I am, and never falsely. The second is, when we are home, nothing will reward you but home itself, and this may be poor recompense, or even brutal. I promise nothing, except to be truthful. And the third thing is, many will die on the return as many died in coming. These will have no monument. Lastly, I am pregnant with the king's child. I hide nothing from you, not even the fact I shall eat better, and sleep warmer than you on these freezing nights. When you see my camp fire burning, you will say, she burns the last wood for herself. I am the queen, and that is so. (*They cheer her.*)

LEAR: How well she speaks! And I said such dishonest things! How well she stands! And I was all gesture and false movements. My friends, I said, my darlings, my brothers and such bollockry, no, she is exemplary, she is, and I should commit suicide!

BISHOP: Never say —

LEAR: I should, and she should govern! What's wrong with suicide? More should contemplate it.

BISHOP: You are a great king.

LEAR: Be careful! Such hyperbole leads to further horror.

BISHOP: A great king and she is shallow.

LEAR: She lacked the benefit of your teaching, which only threw my mind into worse chaos. My head's a sack of clocks, all keeping different hours. **A sack of clocks**. I blame you for this, love and blame you, look at her, she sees through me!

BISHOP: She sees nothing.

LEAR: She sees my incurable sophistication! (*He goes to her.*) I'll speak, shall I? Or not? I thought you exemplary for brevity. No need, I think just —

SOLDIERS: **Lear! Don't go! We saved you, Lear! We crossed a thousand miles of desert and drank foul water**.

LEAR: I burned the houses. I poisoned the wells.

SOLDIERS: **Our guts roared like the drainage of the dungeon and some were sliced by tribesmen. Horribly sliced**. (*They stare at him. With an inspiration, he jumps onto a chair to address them.*)

LEAR: Was going to say —
      But won't now.
      Was going to exaggerate —
      But not now.

Had planned such a speech but now won't give it.
Plaster you with gratitude and effusiveness . . .
But who requires it? (*Pause. They look at him.*)
Or do you . . .?
When I see a crowd I think —
Oh, horror, they expect banality! (*Pause*)
Which you don't, surely? Grey eyes? Bloody paws, and stitched-
together?
Grown out of futile compliments, surely? (*Pause. He searches
their faces.*)
Or not?
Don't want my wet-eyed exhortations, surely?
Want my tiny thanks, great murderers? (*Pause*)
I am certainly the cleverest king that ever lived and this cleverness
I wish I had not, I promise you, but there it is, as some have moles
or a sixth finger I have appalling sight, so you must be patient, **Say
what you want and I'll say it**! (*They start to drift away, unhappily.*)
Who said you could be dismissed? (*They stop, reluctantly.*)
TERRIBLE SOLDIER: Praise us, Lear. (*Pause. They look at him.*)
LEAR: I pat the dog for bringing me my slipper. And hounds who
fetch dead birds. Pat. Pat.
TERRIBLE SOLDIER: But for us you'd be a skin in the enemy's
museum.
LEAR: Ask more of me than thanks. That's easy to give and since
I don't love life —
TERRIBLE SOLDIER: **You don't love life**? (*The shout is violent. The
pause also.*) **He says he don't love life**. (*He looks around.*) **My mates
have things stuck in their eyeballs and He says he don't love life**.
BISHOP (*sotto voce*): Thank them. In any words. But thank them.
TERRIBLE SOLDIER: I buried lovely friends and foes alike and this
one **don't love life**.
BISHOP: Quickly, satisfy them.
LEAR: I merely meant my nature is too philosophical for —
TERRIBLE SOLDIER: **I crawled through burning schools and am one-
eyed for him. And he tells me he does not love his life**. (*Pause. LEAR
looks with a profound hatred at the TERRIBLE SOLDER.*)
LEAR: If you hate me, fight me.
BISHOP: No, no, he is ten times your —
LEAR: Then at least I can keep pure in my language, which is the
heart of me. (*The TERRIBLE SOLDIER unbuckles his belt, which
falls to the floor along with his packs. Taking a knife from his collection,
he flings one to LEAR.*)
BISHOP: He knows nothing of killing . . .!
TERRIBLE SOLDIER: Then why does he make wars? (*The CROWD
roars, and forms a ring of curiosity.*)
CLARISSA: My husband is a child. Tell me if he lives, I refuse to
watch . . . (*She sweeps out. The TERRIBLE SOLDIER stalks LEAR.*)
LEAR: First, I held my ground . . .

And then . . .

I ran in circles! (*He runs. He stops.*)

I thought, I must resort to stratagems. I thought this morally dubious and yet, was not all life likewise dubious? For some seconds I was paralysed by the futility of the ambition to continue to exist. And then — (*Suddenly he lets out a cry and runs, through the watchers. The* TERRIBLE SOLDIER *pursues him off stage. The watchers follow the figures with hand and eyes, groaning or applauding.* HORBLING *squats, not following.*)

HORBLING: The Condolences of History. (*A roar. They point.*) A belief, the holding of which one day appears sheer mischief or eccentricity, on another, shimmers with, rings with, the light of perfect truth. (*They groan.*)

An individual, mocked for his misfortune, acquires, through patience, the attributes of holiness, notwithstanding he hates men. (*They cheer.*)

Your enemy, however great his suffering, and justified in his revenge, will spoil his victory by excess. (*They groan.*)

The oppressor will be pitied, too. (*They cheer.*)

It is a matter of sitting around. (*He cannot contain himself.*)

Kill Him! String his body to the trees! I have the programme! Bury Lear and all his memory! (*He waves the papers. A silence. He has his back to the direction in which* LEAR *enters, wearily. The silence is suggestive. His hand falters. He slips the papers back under his hat. Pause.*)

BISHOP: My son . . . Oh, my son . . .

LEAR: Shh . . .

BISHOP: Oh, my one son . . .

LEAR: Shh . . . (*He is still, allowing no one near him. Pause. The* TERRIBLE SOLDIER, *dying, enters, falls.* LEAR *turns to the body.*)

Oh, awful face, how fate has made a fool of you.

Ridiculous journey of a simple man. (*Suddenly he falls beside the dying man.*)

I want to be good! Get up! I want to be good! (*The watching crowd drifts away as* CLARISSA *returns. She looks at him.*)

CLARISSA: Now we have the child I think . . .

Now you are soon to be a father it must be time. **Suppose he'd killed you**. (*Pause*)

LEAR: You're right. Everything you say is true. Such a clear mind you have, what I wouldn't give for it.

CLARISSA: You congratulate me all the time.

LEAR: Do I?

CLARISSA: Then persist with your —

LEAR: Yes, I do — I —

CLARISSA: So why admire? What's admiration without imitation?

LEAR: What is it, yes, that's indisputable.

CLARISSA: I believe you have a good character but something is obscuring it. (*He nods. She takes his cheeks in both hands.*) Now, call your armourer. We must set off. (*She leaves. The* BISHOP *is alone on the stage with him.*)

BISHOP: How did you win?

LEAR: I appealed to all that was good in him.

BISHOP: Excellent.

LEAR: Which weakened him.

BISHOP: It does.

LEAR: Which made him — anybody's fool. (*The* BISHOP *takes him in his arms. They embrace. A* BOY *enters with armour. The* BISHOP *goes.* LEAR *looks at the* BOY. *Then he stretches his arms.*) If we are to be friends you must be intimate with me. (*The* BOY *begins to armour him.*) I mean by this, keep nothing back, even offensive things you must articulate because secrets are the rot of friendship, aren't they, don't you find? And I will burden you with mine, that is the price of love, it shoulders all else out the road, it's selfish, it is petulant, it rubs the lovers raw. Do you agree?

BOY: Yes ...

LEAR: You are so like me! How you love to care for me. So beautiful the way you tie that sleeve. I think of you a lot. I say a lot, but what's a lot? Always I think of you! What's your name?

BOY: Gary.

LEAR: Oh, I don't like that! Of all the names you might have had, I like that least, but **I must make myself.**

BOY: I could call myself another —

LEAR: No. We cannot turn the world over. We must love it as it is. The helm now. (*The* BOY *puts his helmet on, then runs off. The army begins passing over the stage in its retreat.* LEAR *is quite stationary. The* BISHOP *passes, stops.*)

BISHOP: I found five candlesticks in a burning church. But we must loot. How else can we assuage our impotence? And I'm a bishop! Why do I need candlesticks? (*He goes out. The others pass. At last,* KENT *He stops.*)

KENT: You want to be the last. But I am. (LEAR *doesn't move.*) They say sacrifice is worthless if the object of the sacrifice is itself unworthy. But they who say that don't understand sacrifice. (*Pause. At last* LEAR *moves off.* KENT *follows, the last to leave a devastated country.*)

LEAR*'s Kingdom.* PRUDENTIA.

PRUDENTIA: I wanted my daughter back. Oh, my little daughter. I wanted my daughter dead. Oh, my excellent daughter. I wanted none of them back. Oh, my perfect solitude. I don't know why I like the law so much, I think because it's bottomless, I think because it's interminable, and absolute in five hundred volumes **There a pain can be asphyxiated.** (LEAR *enters, almost on tiptoe.*) A man can lose his hand for theft on Tuesday but not on Saturday. **Don't think that's ridiculous.** On Tuesday he has had time to weigh alternatives, but

by Saturday his morality is tired. You're not dead, then? (*He stops.*)
To be honest I would not care if you — and she too — alive? If
you were three bones in Asia — and I like libraries, they contain
on average one truthful book, but finding it! That's the nightmare,
and truth's a thing you can grow out of, I — (*Pause*)

LEAR: Any other men? (*Pause. Distant sound of parades and rejoicing*)

PRUDENTIA: My health has been good. Every day I walk. And eating
simple food, which is in any case the easiest to find, the shortages
have been most exasperating to a scholar but — (*Pause*)

LEAR: Any other men? (*Pause*)

PRUDENTIA: And I plant roses. Only white. Though white is never
white. My little garden has a dozen whites, all white and yet — (*Pause*)

LEAR: No others, then. (*Pause*)

PRUDENTIA: Take off your shirt. Obsessionist. (*He removes it, slowly.*)
I knew this would be the style of your return. The banners dragging
in the dust. The shuffling feet of the humiliated. And your grin.

LEAR: I burned five towns! (*She looks at him, at last.*)
       I poisoned all their rivers!
       And dragged ploughs through their palaces.

PRUDENTIA: Oh, Lear ... I thrive on your insanity. (*She reaches
out, touches him with the tips of her fingers.*)

LEAR: Tell me I can do no wrong.

PRUDENTIA: All wrongs are right with you.

LEAR: Tell me my excellence.

PRUDENTIA: All you are is excellence.

LEAR: My sin, even?

PRUDENTIA: Even that is grace. (*He laughs, shuddering with relief.
They embrace. GONERIL hurries in.*)

GONERIL: My birth! My birth was far from easy!

CLARISSA *enters, holding her belly.*

CLARISSA: My child comes! (*LEAR and PRUDENTIA skip apart.
A pandemonium of doctors and midwives. A couch.*)

GONERIL: I was reluctant. No, that's understatement. I was recalci-
trant. Even that won't do! **I fixed my heels in her belly and stuck!**

LEAR (*horrified by CLARISSA's pain*): I hate this ...! (*She cries.*) I
hate this ...!

SURGEON: Turn her on her side and throw cold water on her back!

ASSISTANT: (*calling off*): **Cold water!**

GONERIL: I sensed — out there — was **vile.**

LEAR (*wringing his hands*): I hate this ... I hate this!

SURGEON: A dead cat on her stomach!

ASSISTANT (*calling*): **Dead cat!**

LEAR: Is it always like this?

PRUDENTIA (*as a MAN enters with a bucket*): Why a dead cat?

GONERIL: I clung — and yet — hearing my father, thought — how kind his voice is ... (*A bucket of water is thrown over* CLARISSA. *She gasps.*)

PRUDENTIA: A dead cat, why?

SURGEON: **Why not a dead cat! Didn't you require a dead cat?**

PRUDENTIA: Never.

SURGEON: That is your tragedy —

ASSISTANT: Dead cat! (*An animal is carried in.*)

LEAR: I am to blame! I am to blame!

CLARISSA (*in throes of pain*): **You are to blame!**

LEAR: I said so, didn't I!

SURGEON: Face down, now!

PRUDENTIA: **Face down?**

SURGEON: You talk too much! You create a most unhelpful atmosphere in which the miracle of birth can be enjoyed by —

LEAR: **No more love. No more love.**

SURGEON: **Shut up, you are not contributing.**

PRUDENTIA (*holding his hand swiftly*): Go into the garden.

LEAR: Yes. (*He turns to go.*)

SURGEON: We'll save the child. (*He returns to the patient.* LEAR *is struck, his mind races.*)

LEAR: Save the child — then —

PRUDENTIA: **Get this cat off!**

LEAR: Save the child? You mean —

SURGEON (*grappling with* PRUDENTIA): **You are sabotaging this delivery!**

GONERIL (*as they fight over the birth couch*): **A fight at parturition! How could I have been anything but savage?** And yet ... I heard my father ... Suffer ... (*She skips out*)

SURGEON: **I take no further part in this, I retire from all, please witness, I withdraw from all, and deny responsibility for all.** Collect my bag, John we are going home.

ASSISTANT (*going out*): You can easily remarry ... (*The thought penetrates* LEAR.)

LEAR: Obviously I can remarry ... An Asian princess, possibly ... I like their eyes ...

What is to be done with me? I think I am evil! (CLARISSA *and* PRUDENTIA *deliver the child. It gives a first cry*)

Evil because ...

Evil accommodates every idea ...

PRUDENTIA (*bringing the child over*): I think the child wants you ...

LEAR: Me?

PRUDENTIA: Look, it does want you ...! (*He holds it.*)

CLARISSA: Lear ...

LEAR: How beautiful it is! But only beautiful because it owes its life to me ...

CLARISSA: Lear ...!

LEAR: The nature of beauty, as of goodness, rests in its power to substantiate the self . . . Which is not goodness at all, is it? (*He wanders off, thinking, still holding the child*)

CLARISSA: Lear . . .! (CLARISSA *alone with* PRUDENTIA *and a* SERVANT.) Bring my red bird!

PRUDENTIA (*at her side*): Rest, now . . .!

CLARISSA: I think I am living with a murderer!

PRUDENTIA: Shh, now . . .

CLARISSA: All kings are murderers, but **I think I am living with a torturer, bring my red bird!** (The SERVANT *hurries out.*)

PRUDENTIA: Shh . . . shh . . .

CLARISSA: All kings are torturers, but **why do you always apologize for him**? (*Pause*) That is suspicious, though I hate suspicion. And yet it will occur to me no matter what I.

PRUDENTIA: You are so —

CLARISSA: Delirious, of course I am, **have him if you want to. Naked and**. (*Pause. The* SERVANT *brings the cage and places it by her. He goes out.*) That is a terrible accusation, mother. And I uttered it.

PRUDENTIA: Yes.

CLARISSA: Crossing the desert I felt once — so clearly — no one will ever love me.

PRUDENTIA: That's silly, that's —

CLARISSA: No, don't pity me! I don't mean I wept. I was not desolated, I felt — a quality in me forbids it. (*Pause*) A good quality, perhaps. (*Pause*)

PRUDENTIA: I want to hold you, and yet I can't.

CLARISSA: That's funny.

PRUDENTIA: Yes. Believe me when I say I want to hold you.

CLARISSA: Yes, but it makes no sense. (*Pause*) I should sleep now! Perhaps when I wake up I shan't suffer this oppression . . . (*She sleeps.*)

PRUDENTIA: I also want a child . . . are you asleep? I also want a child . . . (*She goes to leave. Semi-darkness, out of which a white plane suddenly descends.*)

FOURTH LEAR

THE GAOL: **Lear**
> **We are familiar with the lies of politicians**
> **Their grins and handshakes we despise**
> **And the freedom fighters**
> **Who trusts their passionate embraces?**
> **Their clenched fists which don't unclench**
> **Look out Freedom's fist in your eyes!**
> **Lear**
> **Our calls must reach your bedroom**
> **On still nights when you sleep alone**
> **The locks locked**
> **The bolts bolted**
> **And the shutters tight**

The moon is walking in the gardens
And we say
Lear is thinking of our pain tonight!
Lear

The white plane descends, in the opposite direction. The BOY *runs in. Dogs bark.*

BOY: Fell there! (*He runs off.*) Fell there! (LEAR *enters, with an* INVENTOR.)

LEAR: Is this with God's permission? Or is it against God?

INVENTOR: He gave us word. He gave us paper. And he gave us curiosity.

LEAR: But not wings.

INVESTOR: Not wings, no.

LEAR: He did not intend us to be birds, or we should be thick with feathers. But does he resent us becoming birds? There is the question.

INVENTOR: He is eager for us to be so. But he requires we ourselves furnish the means. He says, I give you intelligence. Employ it, therefore. The means I will provide, the will you must discover.

LEAR: I have the will.

INVENTOR: He says the earth is a most imperfect place, go forth and tidy it.

LEAR: Yes.

INVENTOR: After all, did He not have a mere seven days to make it?

LEAR: No time at all.

INVENTOR: He knew even the infant would place his finger in the caterpillar's path. Why? To observe how it altered its behaviour. So every man inflicts himself on his terrain. The horse is placed in shafts. The peasant turns the water's course to his advantage. And even in the death cell the prisoner tutors the mouse. God smiles at this. God claps. (*The* BOY *appears holding the damaged plane.*)

BOY: Busted.

LEAR: Correct its faults. (*The* INVENTOR *bows.*)
    Then make the full-sized version. (*He bows again.*)
    I'll fly myself. (*He goes out.* LEAR *seizes the* BOY *in an embrace.*)
    Here's peace! Here's goodness, surely? Here's truth without contradiction?

BOY: You're hurting me . . . (LEAR *looks at him. Pause.*) Yes . . . (KENT *enters. The* BOY *runs out.*)

LEAR: Ah, I do so hate to see you sometimes. Always grave. Always responsible. I never had an uncle but you must be what uncles look like. I never had a friend, but you must be what friends aspire to. You are going to reprimand me. (*Pause*) Or shall I make the speech? I could.

KENT: Everything is neglected.

LEAR: Yes.

KENT: To take a single example, the roads are pits.

LEAR: The people move too much. Look at all these accidents.

KENT: I beg you to be —

LEAR: **People must keep still**. (*Pause*)

What connection is there between movement and knowledge? None, I promise you. Anything else?

KENT: The river burst its banks.

LEAR: It's the rain does it.

KENT: Obviously, but —

LEAR: If we control the river, we shall control the lake.

If we control the lake we shall control the weather.

If we control the weather we shall abolish rain, for no one likes to get his head wet. Then we shall starve. No, it's better we endure floods.

KENT: We? The castle's on a hill.

LEAR: It is much closer to the lightning.

KENT: **All these unnecessary deaths**!

LEAR: Unnecessary deaths? And what is a necessary one?

KENT: **You irritate my loyalty with such fatuous** —

LEAR: **And you my patience with inanity**! (*Pause*)

No, we must be friends. Mustn't we? If friends we are.

KENT: I think, Lear, in your case, there is no fitting the hand of intelligence into the glove of government.

LEAR: None. And I gave you the chance to kill me in the desert ... (KENT *walks away*.) They say you are a nice man! But wouldn't a nice man kill me, in order to be nice to others? (*A thin bells rings. A pair of* BEGGARS *enter, one mute*.)

Hey! Two of my happy subjects! What, brothers, no clinic? No warm house? No hot dinners? There's the man! Protest! (*He points to* KENT.)

He says you should not die — unnecessarily! (KENT *goes out in disgust*.)

I feel you ought to live to ninety, but what's ninety? No, that's unjust, seven hundred would be better, **ugh, that sore is vile** ...! (*He turns in horror, then slowly, turns back and compels himself to examine it. The* BEGGAR *rings the bell*.)

You have the sore ... I have the coin ... I give you the coin ... you still have the sore ... (*He holds out money*.)

BEGGAR: Give you the sore with pleasure.

LEAR (*as the* BEGGAR *pockets the coin*): Do you believe in anything?

BEGGAR: Yes. Tomorrow.

LEAR: Is that so? I fear tomorrow. I fear tomorrow I may doubt the few things I succeeded in believing in today. (*The* BEGGAR *sets off*.)

Don't go I'm the monarch. (*They stop*.)

I do think it's funny, that you and I have nothing in common. Less even than a cow and a crow. Or a worm and a horse. Less than them, even.

BEGGAR: They share the field, at least.

LEAR: They share the field, yes. (*The* BEGGAR *sets off with a ring of his bell.*)

    Don't go I'll stab you! (*They stop.*)

BEGGAR: I'll starve to death if I must listen to your logic —

LEAR (*cruelly*): **I need it. As you need bread, I need it**. (*Pause. The* BEGGAR *shrugs.*)

BEGGAR: At least give us another coin. (LEAR *spins one.*)

LEAR: I'm sure we must have one thing in common. Don't we? **One thing**?

BEGGAR: I shit.

LEAR: Yes, well there is a beginning.

BEGGAR: And piss.

LEAR: There's another, but don't be coarse I'll have your tongue out. This is a polite society.

BEGGAR: I was born, and I must die.

LEAR: The first yes, the second we don't know yet.

BEGGAR: Must die, obviously.

LEAR: **What's obvious about it**? (*Pause. He spins another coin.*)

    All we know is that all others die. From that it cannot be deduced we also shall. Perhaps you are immortal. It would be like immortality to bestow itself on something so grotesque and unbenign as you.

    Don't ring the bell, I'm talking. (*Pause. The* BEGGAR *is patient.*) How greedy you are. I have already given more than you could hope to beg in seven days and far from creating in you a sense of gratitude you are ringing now from pure avarice! (*Pause. The* BEGGAR *is so uncomfortable under* LEAR's *examining gaze, he fumbles for the money in his pockets and flings it down.*)

BEGGAR: I can't stick this! Take it! Can I go now, monarch? (*The coin rolls over the floor. The* BEGGARS *get up to go.*)

LEAR: A duke has died without an heir. Of some place known as Gloucester.

BEGGAR: Tramped there . . .

LEAR: Good. You are his successor. (*Pause. The* BEGGAR *stares at* LEAR.)

BEGGAR: What is this? Torture?

LEAR: **You think you are the only one who's tortured?** (*A smile comes over the* BEGGAR's *face. He grasps his mute companion.*) Not him.

BEGGAR: I've tramped with him eleven years.

LEAR: This is a journey you must make alone.

BEGGAR: He has no tongue and — (LEAR, *mocking dumbness, shakes his head. A pause of sufficient brevity. Then the* BEGGAR *disburdens himself of his bags and satchels and drapes his companion with them. He kisses him swiftly on the cheek and gives him the bell. The* CHORUS *enters.*)

LEAR: Let no one say I hide things from myself.

THE GAOL: **Lear**

LEAR: Let no one say I do not see all sides of the argument.

THE GAOL: **Lear**

LEAR: All consequences and connections.

THE GAOL: **Lear**

LEAR: Ramifications and —

THE GAOL: **Lear**

LEAR: I had not forgotten you. One whim could liberate you. So small an action on my part. And yet. (*An effect of sound and light. An airplane is revealed.*) For this a hundred children starved. For this, four thousand went without arithmetic. And groves of soft fruit perished ... (*The* BOY *enters holding* LEAR's *flying kit.* LEAR *extends his hands for the gloves.* PRUDENTIA *enters. She looks at him.*)

INVENTOR: The wings rotate at seven revolutions to the minute, the mean average of the herring gull. The thickness of the air will cause the craft to float as boats do on water and possibly you may effect a landing on the clouds, the upper sides of which it is believed by us contain estates of lush cultivation.

PRUDENTIA: My body is a better medium to move in, did I not praise you enough, I am forever praising you, this is an affront to me, this is a criticism, or rather a pique, a little criticism worthy of an infant and not a solution.

GONERIL (*entering*): Do go, and hurry, I love you!

PRUDENTIA: The things you have called me, the abuse and the superlatives, my coarse hound, you raised me up against the factory gates one night, there was flight if ever flight was.

GONERIL: And bring me something!

PRUDENTIA: **Have I no power over you!**

GONERIL: Something big and lovely!

PRUDENTIA: I shan't plead! I shan't wheedle! If you fall dying to the ground I'll put up my skirts and piss your face with anger, do you hear me? Do take the gauntlets off you look an idiot but I'm the only one who'll tell you, it takes love to properly humiliate, die for all I care, but not absurdly, please, it mocks me also ...! (CLARISSA *enters, pregnant with* REGAN.)

CLARISSA: Don't fly.

PRUDENTIA: He flies because he hates us.

GONERIL: Be quiet, I want a present!

CLARISSA: Don't fly.

LEAR: If I discover paradise, I shan't come back. At least until I discover paradise is wanting. Kiss me all those who loved me, and the rest, pretend. (*The* COURTIERS *gather round, but* PRUDENTIA *and* CLARISSA *remain still.*)

LEAR: Clarissa, always you make me feel ashamed. And to escape shame, I try to rise above it ...

GONERIL: Oh, do go and hurry! (*The* INVENTOR *goes to a wing, the* BOY *to another. A drum is tapped.* LEAR, *in the pilot's seat, cranks a handle to the rhythm.* GLOUCESTER, *the elevated beggar, appears resplendent. He goes to* HORBLING.)

GLOUCESTER: On Thursday I was a tramp, on Friday I fucked rich women. There's a joke, surely? Don't tell the other tramps! (*He goes to* PRUDENTIA.) Have you a lover?

PRUDENTIA: I am learning to go without one.

GLOUCESTER: Excellent. (*He goes to* CLARISSA.) And you?

CLARISSA: I led an army into Asia . . .

GLOUCESTER: I saw them. They were on the bridge and I was underneath it.

CLARISSA: I led an army into Asia . . .

GLOUCESTER: So you said, but I would love to see your belly.

CLARISSA: **For this** . . .! (*The drum beat rises.* LEAR *cranks faster.*)

HORBLING: The king became a bird, have you heard this one? The king stuck feathers on himself. And the queen said — **I so hate comedy it makes men cruel!** (*The cranking and the drumming reach a climax at the end of which* LEAR *falls exhausted over the handles. The drumming slows, the wings cease to flap. In the stillness,* GLOUCESTER *goes to the* DRUMMER, *takes his sticks, and tosses them onto the floor.*)

GONERIL: Oh, he is not perfect, my father . . .! (CLARISSA *goes to her child. She puts her hands on her shoulders.*)

CLARISSA: Lear wished to fly, and could not. And I wish to be happy, and cannot. Always less. Less always. In lessness we must discover plenitude. Less always. Always less. (LEAR *climbs off the plane and flings himself to the ground. He flattens himself, as if struggling to be drawn into the earth. He writhes. He moans.*)

INVENTOR: It's weight.

CLARISSA: **It is not weight it's purpose.**

INVENTOR: The king, though much reduced by fasting, also reduced his energy, thereby demolishing the ratio of power to wing area —

KENT: Shh . . .

INVENTOR: The necessary combination can be achieved by —

KENT: Shh . . . (*He goes to usher the* INVENTOR *away.*)

LEAR: My boy is light . . . (*They stop.* LEAR *straightens himself onto his knees. Pause.*)

CLARISSA: Lear, accept the sign.

LEAR (*to the* BOY): You're light, aren't you?

CLARISSA: Accept the sign, that also is a proof of wisdom.

LEAR: **Sil-ence!** (*He blocks his ears. Pause.*)

BOY: I'll go. But I'll be late for dinner! (*Pause.* LEAR *gets to his feet.*)

LEAR: We'll keep some back.

INVENTOR (*moving to the wings*): Drummer!

CLARISSA: Oh, you are intolerable to a kind mind!

LEAR: **And you are a guillotine on lips or fingers!** (CLARISSA *takes* GONERIL *out.*)
      Steel mouth and steel body! (*Pause. The* BOY *climbs up on the plane.*)

BOY: Ready!

INVENTOR: Drum! (*The* DRUMMER *beats the cranking rhythm. The* INVENTOR *and another return to the wings. A wind. The* BOY *cranks.*

LEAR *hurries forward as a torrent of feathers descends over the stage, obliterating the plane.*)

LEAR: Oh, who loves kings!

Oh, who loves thrones, somebody must!

THE GAOL: **Ha, ha, ha, ha, ha, ha!**

LEAR: Oh, kneel before his severed head, it was so full of passion once!

THE GAOL: **Ha, ha, ha, ha, ha, ha!**

LEAR: The temper of the underdog has its own beauty, but so has the firing squad! (*Silence. The last feathers fall. Sound of the wind. Nobody moves. Their eyes scan upwards.*)

HORBLING: If ever there was need for humour this is. (*Pause*)

Since no one else will I. (*Pause*)

At certain times only an idiot can find the words so. (*Pause*)

His ineptitude uncannily fills the need of. (*Pause*)

For example, at Golgotha, there was an idiot. This idiot danced under Christ whilst. (*Pause. The clothing of the* BOY *falls out of the sky at* LEAR'*s feet*)

Lear has killed his one loved boy! (*He points at* LEAR.)
There is the cause of all our discontent so.
Accuse him!

Overthrow! (*No one moves.* HORBLING *rubs his face ruefully.* LEAR *picks up the clothing.*)

LEAR: He did not love me. But when I instructed him, he repeated the words. (*He looks around.*) What more can you ask?

GLOUCESTER (*coming to him*): Let's adjourn to a silent room, and ask an old woman to dance naked . . .

LEAR: Why . . .?

GLOUCESTER: Or row a skiff to the madhouse on the rocks . . .

LEAR: Why . . .? (GLOUCESTER *shrugs*.) It is not life that's sacred. It is death.

INVENTOR (*picks up a fragment*): The structure of the rudder seems —

LEAR: Did he have time to make his death?

INVENTOR: If anything, too flexible, which is not difficult to —

LEAR: His lost years are nothing but could he make his own death, or did you deprive him? (*The* INVENTOR *looks uncomfortable.*)

INVENTOR: It is the story of our progress. Grief, and after grief, design. The graveyard and the drawing board.

LEAR: Yes. But we must live our own deaths, and not be cheated. You robbed him with your accident. (*The* INVENTOR *looks to* KENT, *anxiously*.) Lock this criminal away, and keep him penciless. For if he has a pencil, he will invent. And no twigs either, or he'll make charcoal. It is a disease, this rabid invention. (*Pause. Then* KENT *goes, reluctantly, to arrest the* INVENTOR.) You shuffle, which is a mute criticism of instruction.

KENT: Perhaps you know things which a simple man like me —

LEAR: Come, come, you, simple?

KENT: A man of rather plain intelligence —

LEAR: You, plain? Never. Why this incessant apology, you bolt apology to yourself like armour, and you love my wife. (*Pause.* KENT *drags the* INVENTOR *offstage.*

PRUDENTIA (*going to him*): Make love to me, you wretched, lonely man.

LEAR: Tuck up your skirt for Gloucester, he has more appetite.

PRUDENTIA: Have you no love for me? **I am so glad you are not dead**.

LEAR: It's shallow . . .

PRUDENTIA: Let it be shallow. **So glad**.

LEAR: It was a lake, and now it is a pool. Soon, it will be a puddle, and the sun will boil it to a dark stain on the pavement.

PRUDENTIA: I have been too loyal.

LEAR: Who knows?

PRUDENTIA: I have made myself a casual possession.

LEAR: Who knows? And once I lay all night on a roof to watch you dressing.

PRUDENTIA: I have no dignity. Come with me. I have no pride.

LEAR: And that's a freedom . . . (*He puts a hand on her.*)

> I am waiting to be killed, and no one does it. (*She takes him in her arms. He clings to her.*)

INTERLUDE

The sea shore. The BISHOP *paddles, lifting his robe.*

THE GAOL: **How excellent
To be the executed
How excellent
To know you caused offence
How painful to be just
The victim of an accident
A piece of historic inconsequence**

**How good to be an executioner
That also is a skill
Ask those who suffered from the inept
How good to be an executioner
He walks home with a civic sense**

KENT *Enters, and watches the* BISHOP *from a distance.*

BISHOP (*sensing him*): I have these feet.
> And salt relieves them.
> Sometimes the feet are twice the size.
> Pity me. I do. (*He paddles.*)

The sea!

Sometimes it kills, and sometimes it cures.

Pity me I haven't long to live.

KENT: Nobody likes you.

BISHOP: It's true. I always seem to be thinking something else. Behind good-morning even, there is an altogether different sentiment. No one likes this, naturally.

KENT: They say you spoiled the king.

BISHOP: Yes, and what are you, the vessel of opinion or do you have a —

> **Oh you have a knife**
> **He has a knife fancy**
> **Fancy**
> **He has a knife**

And look at me, too far from anyone, oh, I have chosen a silly time to bathe, no what is your view, or are you just the vessel of opinion? Chuck us a towel.

KENT: Unnecessary.

BISHOP: What, the towel?

KENT: Unnecessary, yes.

BISHOP: Oh, dear, never to have dry feet again. This is the last time I shall get near a vessel of opinion. Who are you doing this for? Everybody? I do love that! You are smothering your personal dislike of violence in the interests of the community. I do love that. Give us a towel.

KENT: No towel.

BISHOP: Time to get rid of the Bishop. Ask Kent. He's free. Seen Kent? I know someone who can stick a knife in. Kent, you mean? Yes, him, but say it's for the people. Oh, Kent, you're in, everybody hates the Bishop, got ten minutes? **Kent you have no interior sight and you pass that off as goodness.** (*Pause.* KENT *takes out his knife.*)

KENT: You have to die.

BISHOP: Only me?

KENT: I think so, yes.

BISHOP: Only me. Relax, you other criminals. Only me . . . (*Two children appear*, GONERIL *and* REGAN.)

GONERIL/REGAN: 'ello, 'ello! 'ello!

KENT: Go away. Your mother wants you.

GONERIL/REGAN: 'ello, 'ello, 'ello!

BISHOP: **Come here, dearies**!

KENT: Oh, you loathsome man . . .

BISHOP: Yes, but I must be consistent.

GONERIL: What are you doing here?

BISHOP: Not a lot.

REGAN: You don't go to the beach, do you?

BISHOP: No, this is my final visit.

GONERIL: Mummy says steer clear of you.

BISHOP: Difficult, up till now. But from tomorrow, easy. **That's enough**

wit, this man is out to murder me! (*Pause. The* CHILDREN *stare, open-mouthed. Then they hold hands.*)

REGAN: Swim, then. That way.

KENT: How loathsome, to drape yourself in children.

BISHOP: Yes, how loathsome I appear to want to live. I appear to be prepared to annexe anything to hand to perpetuate my miserable life. How loathsome. I really need examining.

GONERIL: Swim for a day and you get to an island.

BISHOP: I haven't a day, unfortunately. (*Swiftly, he grabs* REGAN, *thrusting her body in front on him.*)

REGAN: Ow! Mummy!

KENT: Oh, you nauseaous and —

GONERIL (*rushing off*): Mummy! Mummy!

BISHOP: Oh, vile thing I am, vile bag of wicked thought and physical corruption, I am so ashamed! (*Pause. Gulls cry.* REGAN *is stiff and white.*)

KENT: If I doubted the rightness of this murder, this action must confirm it.

BISHOP: Hilarious. Your logic. Hilarious.

REGAN: He'll kill me by mistake!

BISHOP: Well, yes, I think he will. He is a man of real convictions, **don't move**. (*Pause. The* CHILD *stares. At last, the* BISHOP *pushes her away. She wanders, then runs off.*) How magnificent the gestures of the bad ... I did that, not out of love of infants, who are nothing, but because one day I think she will hunt you ... (KENT *goes to him, kills him. The* BISHOP *sinks into the water.* CLARISSA *appears, controlling her horror.*)

CLARISSA: I never thought I would give thanks for murder, but I must not hide behind the fiction that all life is good. How simple that would be. How simple and intransigent. Such absolute moralities are frequently the refuge of misanthropy ...

KENT (*roping up the body*): Any thought that Lear produced, this man legitimized.

CLARISSA: **We must protect the weak against the cunning**. (*Pause.* KENT *stops, looks at her.*)

KENT: Yes ... (*The* CHILDREN *call, off, she goes, swiftly.*)

THE GAOL: **Oh Kent**
            You excellent and permanently servile mind.

KENT: The tide ...

THE GAOL: **Even your worst enemy you bury**.

KENT: How swift this tide is!

THE GAOL: **Your mother taught you manners and you can't forget**
            Your father said to tell the truth and open doors for women

KENT: Hey! (*A high wind lashes the stage.*) He floats! His corpse is a balloon of gases! (*He clings to the body of the* BISHOP. *Music, which stops with a burst of sunlight.* KENT *climbs off the body.*) God help me ... I am on a rock ... a fucking rock ... and oh ... **Nobody**!

BISHOP: There's me ...

KENT: No sticks to burn ... no fruit to eat ... **Oi! I railed Oi!** I railed, and then I sat, for standing was pointless. And then lay, for sitting was pointless ... (*He lies. The sun beats down. His hand goes to his crotch.*) Clarissa ... If three matrons stood between you and my cock I'd savage them **anybody listening!** (*The sea*) Clarissa ... I would bend you across my knee and stare into your cavity ... **Anybody listening!** (*The sea*)

BISHOP: Sun ... surely?

KENT: I would walk over the mouths of the world's poor to grasp you by the —

BISHOP: Salt water, obviously ...

KENT (*prodding the body*): **Get back!** (*The* BISHOP *laughs*) Get back (*Pause*)

I pushed it away, but back it came, on every tide ... my superior in perception ...

FIFTH LEAR

A hammering at a door. LEAR, *bearded, on a bed. A window, with a number of kites outside, flying, indicating the height of the room.* HOR-BLING *enters.*

HORBLING: I knock. But that's a formality. I have permission. Permission, and more permission. For what? What's permission if imagination's dead? (*He goes to* LEAR.) Are you asleep? I bring petitions. From the inventor, asking for his sentence to be halved? And the rest are from the inveterately cruel. They give them to me because Kent's missing. By the time I reach the top of the stairs I am carrying my own weight in paper. (*He drops a pile of petitions on the floor. He watches the kites move.*) Why don't you give them bread? I don't understand it. There is enough bread. You get the loaf and you go — (*He pretends to break it.*) Two people fed! And you take the two halves and you — (*He mimes breaking them again.*) Four people fed! I really do not understand — (PRUDENTIA *enters.*)

PRUDENTIA: Weren't you the minister under the old king?

HORBLING: Me?

PRUDENTIA: Yes. Horbling, wasn't it?

HORBLING: I don't think so. Or was I? Oh, yes, but briefly! (LEAR *sits up. The sound of metallic footsteps outside.*) What's that? (*They come nearer.*) Your assassins, I presume ...? (*Two armoured* FIGURES *appear in the door.* HORBLING *rushes to them.*) There he sits! Eliminate the bloody oppressor of widows and orphans! Strike and. (*He stops. He sits.* LEAR *comes to the figures, and looks at them. They begin to shake, with laughter.*)

GONERIL/REGAN: Oh, Dad, our hearts ache for you! (*They throw off their helmets.*)

REGAN: Such trickery to reach our father, so immured is he in his tower!

GONERIL: But love will always find a way!

REGAN: Love does!

GONERIL: Love will!

GONERIL/REGAN: Love always — (*They revolve in an embrace, stop.*)

REGAN: Why is our mother's mother here?

GONERIL: We reach our non-existent dad and —

REGAN: Why is our mother's mother here? (*Pause.* PRUDENTIA *moves to the bed, and sits.*)

GONERIL (*bursting with pleasure again*): We were going to sing you a song!

REGAN: We learned a song!

GONERIL: But now we're too happy to sing! Do you admire us?

REGAN: We're women of **exceptional initiative** you must admit! (*She kisses* LEAR.)

GONERIL: We're giggling!

REGAN: We're frothing!

GONERIL/REGAN: **How clever to get past the guards**!

REGAN: Do we embarrass you!

GONERIL/REGAN: **Pair of idiots**! (*He holds them to his chest.*)

GONERIL: I passed my exams!

REGAN: And I learned archery!

GONERIL: I can swim the rivers both ways!

REGAN: Boys we hate

GONERIL: But horses!

REGAN: We're giggling!

GONERIL: We're frothing!

GONERIL/REGAN: **We embarrass him**! (*A pause. He examines them.*)

REGAN: How warm your hands are, like loved garments ... and the smell ... (*She kisses his hands.*)

LEAR: Every moment I yielded up to love ... is lost to my own struggle ...

GONERIL (*peering into him*): What struggle ...?

REGAN: Look, his feet point inwards till ...!

LEAR: Every excellence of intimacy broke the thin wire of my concentration ...

GONERIL: Yes ...?

LEAR: I wish to be a saint, and all your charm, and love, and small, round voices, washed like a babbling stream the mortar from the joints of my great arch, I want to be a saint and more so that a father ...

GONERIL/REGAN: Yes, yes! And that is why we love you!

REGAN: We said that together!

GONERIL/REGAN: **Do ignore us if you wish!**

GONERIL: And that, too!

PRUDENTIA: I encouraged him. In every thing, I encouraged him. Because he is a great man.

HORBLING: She says so, but where's the evidence? She asserts it, but where's the proof? If he is great why are the poor poor? This tower is so tall their dying groans don't reach him.

PRUDENTIA: Yes, he is a perfect man, and you screech like a duck drowned by its companions.

REGAN: Why is our mother's mother here?

GONERIL: She cleans does she?

REGAN: She makes the beds?

HORBLING: Makes the beds untidy, yes, by manoeuvring upon her arse. **Don't punish it's all in the past**, as the killer said to the widow.

GONERIL: Why does the king like you?

HORBLING: Good question. He brought me up this tower and gave me a spoon. That may be fondness, that may be not. If A is sent to gaol and invites B to join him, is that friendship? Ponder. Ponder. If B refuses, is that bad manners?

LEAR (*to his daughters*): Leave us now. You've grown, that's obvious. Whether you're beautiful is for other men to judge, and whether you're intelligent is insignificant, for if you're not, others will be.

GONERIL: You once ran with me the length of the sea-shore. I've never forgotten that.

LEAR: I loved you insanely. But in loving you insanely, I only loved myself.

REGAN: Come out and govern the world.

PRUDENTIA: He had a teacher, but now he teaches himself.

GONERIL/REGAN: **What is our mother's mother doing here**? (*Lights change. The* CHORUS *are seen holding the kite strings and staring up*.)

THE GAOL: **For every child that dies we fly a kite**
   Lear
   Are you not blind with kites?
   For every suicide that leaps into the river
   We fly a kite
   Lear
   How dark your room must be!

CLARISSA *enters, holding a loud-hailer. She puts it to her lips.*

CLARISSA: I most tenderly wish to see you
 I most anxiously want to touch you.
 I married you.
 I saved you from your enemies.
 I will not be dissuaded from you no matter what indifference you show.
 My bird is dead but I have learned his patience.
 And if you hate my voice it is no more than I hate it myself.

Pause. The strings move in the wind. She gives the loud hailer to a MAN *He proceeds to reiterate her speech.*

MAN: She most tenderly wishes to see you. She most anxiously wants to touch you. She married you. She saved you from your enemies. She will not be dismissed from you no matter what indifference you show. Her bird is dead but she has learned his patience And if you hate her voice, it is no more than she hates it herself. (*He walks to a new spot to repeat the message.*

CLARISSA: Every day I'm here. Every day the message seems less true. But it is not less true merely from being repeated. (REGAN *and* GONERIL *appear, elated.*)

GONERIL/REGAN: **We saw him!**

GONERIL: And he is beautiful!

REGAN: He wears black!

GONERIL: Aged a little —

REGAN: Considerably aged!

GONERIL: Considerably aged yes —

REGAN: But silent!

GONERIL: Almost —

REGAN: Almost silent, yes —

GONERIL/REGAN: **And there is a woman there who looks as if.** (GLOU-CESTER *enters.*)

GLOUCESTER: I go to the brothel. I do not expect to be happy in the brothel. But there at least I am able to suffocate the question whether I am happy or not. (*He looks up.*) What does he do up there? (*He goes out*)

CLARISSA (*to her MAN*): When she comes down, my mother, hood her, and in the hood, bring her to me. Do it if she cries or struggles. But hood her. (*He bows.*) **I mean however painful do it**. (*He goes out. She looks to* GONERIL *and* REGAN *half-afraid. But they are bland.*)

GONERIL: What kind of grandmother was that?

REGAN: She never played with us.

GONERIL/REGAN: **At that age you surely should be nice!** (*They run out.* CLARISSA *looks at the* CHORUS *of the poor, as they pluck their kite strings, moving together like tillers of a field.*)

CLARISSA: I so hate lies. But, look, the poor! (*She looks at them silently moving.*) I so hate subterfuge. But, look, the destitute! (*She looks. She hurries away. A clang.* PRUDENTIA *hooded is brought in by* TWO MEN.)

PRUDENTIA: It's all right, I can walk! Oh, let me walk! Why drag me when I have —

FIRST MAN: **Legs!**

PRUDENTIA: Legs, yes —

SECOND MAN: **We see your legs!**

FIRST MAN: And wonder —

SECOND MAN: **Where have they been, those legs?**

FIRST MAN: **Where have they thrashed the sky, don't we?** (*They place her on a stool. Pause.*) The pleasure it give us to grab a lawyer. We were so abused by you in courts. You and your vocabulary. You and your wit.

BOTH MEN: **You called us things and it stuck like spit to our expressions. Admit our pleasure. No human could resist**. (*Pause. They stand back from her.*)

PRUDENTIA: Do you know who I am?

FIRST MAN: Yes.

PRUDENTIA: Do you realise the perilous position you have placed yourselves in?

SECOND MAN: We realise your legal language is quite dead.

FIRST MAN: Oh, immaculately exercised legs. Grandmother ... (*They creep away, silently. CLARISSA appears. Pause.*)

CLARISSA: Oh, mother, thank you for years of love ... (*She collapses onto another stool, holding her head in her hands. Pause.*) I must leave you hooded because if your eyes meet mine, no thing that is correct could be articulated ...

PRUDENTIA: Take it off.

CLARISSA: Your eyes would make all crime like passing showers.

PRUDENTIA: Remove it, then.

CLARISSA: Precisely what I cannot for the reasons I have just —

PRUDENTIA: Excellent reasons.

CLARISSA: Are they, though?

PRUDENTIA: Yes, it's truth which burns out argument.

CLARISSA: **I will not have you uncovered all my life I have been dominated. Words. Axes. Looks. Clubs**. (*Pause*) Pity me, because this is so difficult.

PRUDENTIA: I pity nobody.

CLARISSA: **Not even the poor**.

PRUDENTIA: Not even them. (*Pause*)

CLARISSA: You have been seized because — (*She stops, shakes her head.*) No, I seized you. I did. Because things can't go on.

PRUDENTIA: They can if no one puts an end to them.

CLARISSA: They can't go on and —

PRUDENTIA: **No one has to act**. (*Pause*) This acting. This intervening. This putting stops to things. Who obliges you, Clarissa?

CLARISSA: My conscience.

PRUDENTIA: Put it to sleep, then. Strike it with a shovel. Like a senile dog, one swift and clean blow kills it. I was spun by conscience like a top. And when it died I came to life. The top ceased spinning. Look how you shiver. Look how manifestly you are inferior to me. Do I shiver? You are in the blindfold.

CLARISSA: **I think you lie in bed with my husband and** — (*She shakes her head like a cat in a bag.*)

> No!
> No!
> Do what you wish, I am not censorious, do what comes

to you, but out there is all starvation and mismanagement and you encourage him!

PRUDENTIA: I could have read this diatribe off any wall.

CLARISSA: Yes.

PRUDENTIA: When a child dies they fly a black rag.

CLARISSA: Yes.

PRUDENTIA: And for every suicide a white.

CLARISSA: You notice, then?

PRUDENTIA: You think the recitation of their agony could alter his pursuit? The sky could be thick in kites and the sun dead. (*Pause*)

CLARISSA: I think your passion, which was magnificent, perhaps, has gone misshapen with obsession, and your love has failed, for love must also be correction —

PRUDENTIA: Ha!

CLARISSA: Yes, love says because I love you I forbid you this or this —

PRUDENTIA: Ha!

CLARISSA: Ha! as much as you like, I am not deterred — a proper love is a matter of fine balances —

PRUDENTIA: **Fine balances**.

CLARISSA: And equilibrium —

PRUDENTIA: **Equilibrium**!

CLARISSA: Yes! And how you hate those things, how you strangle the clean things in yourself —

PRUDENTIA: **This is clean.** (*Pause*)

        Shh!

        That's him! He calls me from the tower! (*She stands, head tilted.*)

CLARISSA: I think you are guilty. Of smothering your self. Which also is a murder.

PRUDENTIA: He is a great man, and I gave him birth. More so than his mother. (CLARISSA *sobs violently.*)

CLARISSA: How your reproaches twist my stomach, and pulp my little heart ... (LEAR's *distant cry is heard. In a spontaneous gesture*, PRUDENTIA *reaches out her hands to* CLARISSA. CLARISSA *does not accept them.*) *No love without criticism*! (*She looks at her mother.* PRUDENTIA's *hands fall.*) And I must see you. I must not hide. (*She pulls away* PRUDENTIA's *blindfold. She stoops in front of her, looking into her eyes.*)

        How hard this is.

        But I.

        And I.

        Can.

THE GAOL: **Oh, good!**

        She's evil if the word has meaning

        Oh, good!

        We do hate punishment but some it must be said

        Deserve

        Oh, good!

        In this case human dignity cries out for

        One of those rare occasions when everybody must

        Agree

Collectively we must respond
Mustn't we

An effect of sound.

LEAR *runs in to an empty stage, bright as day.* GLOUCESTER *is shambling.*

LEAR: Hey!

GLOUCESTER: Shh, I'm depressed ...

LEAR: Have you seen a woman?

GLOUCESTER: I'm so depressed ...

LEAR: In a red skirt and —

GLOUCESTER: **I'm too depressed**. (*He sits.* LEAR *sees another.*)

LEAR: Hey! (*The* FIGURE *stops.*) Have you seen a woman?

HERDSMAN: What do you want a woman for?

LEAR: I want her because — (*He ponders.*) I no longer have her.

HERDSMAN: But when you had her —

LEAR: None of your peasant wisdom. I am Lear. Nothing you can tell me I did not already know at birth. She wore a red skirt.

HERDSMAN: I could have been a monarch. I was born in the wrong room however. (*He laughs coarsely.*)

LEAR (*going close to him*): I said none of your profundity you ambling and complacent self-regarding parcel of banality, if she's dead I also with to die. (*Pause*)

HERDSMAN: She is.

LEAR: She is, is she?

HERDSMAN: The king's whore's dead.

LEAR: The king's whore, yes, that is the one I am referring to. The slag. The man-lover whose parted limbs are ridiculed in public places.

HERDSMAN: Dead yes, what more can I say?

LEAR: No more. Now murder me.

HERDSMAN: I would, except it's treason.

LEAR: I give you permission, here. (*He scrawls on a scrap of paper.*) Command, it says, and that's my signature.

HERDSMAN: I'd rather not.

LEAR: Piss your preference, do it, here's the knife.

HERDSMAN: Look, there's Jack over there —

LEAR: Fuck Jack, you are the chosen — (*He thrusts the knife into the* HERDSMAN's *hand.*)

HERDSMAN: There are more women than — (LEAR *seizes him by the throat.*)

LEAR: **Liar! He tells me there are more women than one! Liar! There was only one**! (*The* HERDSMAN *wriggles free and runs.*) Thrash him for lying! Break him on some wheel for lying! I never lie! Every word I look at, both from the front and the back ... ! (*Pause*)

GLOUCESTER: I go to the brothel. I say to the girl, act naturally. As if I were repulsive to you. 'You, repulsive?', she says. **You are**

such a bad interpreter of my needs, I say, with an artificial grin. I
do detest you. I do resent your ignorance. If I wanted love, I'd find
it . . . (KENT *enters, slowly. He looks at* LEAR.)

KENT: I have been six years on a rock.

LEAR: And I six in a tower.

KENT: I thought of a woman. This kept me sane.

LEAR: And I through one. This maddened me.

HERDSMAN (*returning*): Changed my mind. I thought, I'll do this.
How my neighbours still congratulate me. Michael, they'll say, it is
a privilege to shake your bloody hand. Wash it never.

LEAR: Too late.

HERDSMAN: No, surely? (LEAR *goes to him, and swiftly kills him.*)
Hey . . .! (LEAR *goes out.*)

KENT: **The things we quarrelled over now seem**
The things we stabed for suddenly aren't
The books we carried high
Are only
Fit for arse paper

The genius we thought had understood reality
His eighty volumes now I say are
His beard I wish
His tomb I could

The little man from China with the answers
Was a torturer I never knew
I never knew
I never knew
Did you

And the poet in the tower who we called a
Fucking snob

Has relevance

SIXTH LEAR

A table. CLARISSA, GONERIL, REGAN *seated.* LEAR *enters. He
looks into her. Pause.*

LEAR: Nearly stupid. (*Pause*)
But not quite. (*Pause*)
I am shedding thought as a lout shakes scurf. (*He scratches
his head violently, stops.*) Nearly fit to govern. (CLARISSA *extends
a hand to him across the table.*) I killed a man and Kent's back. (*Ignoring
her hand he sits. The table is an image of domestic silence. Her hand
remains until it agonizes her.*)

GONERIL: Oh, take that hand back . . .!

REGAN: Mother! (*It stays, until at last she falls into her chair, her eyes on the floor.*)

CLARISSA: I can't apologize for what was proper. Or that's madness. But for pain. I share that. (*She looks at* LEAR, *who extends his arms over the table, so his hands reach for his children, his cheek to the table. They take his hands. They look at their mother. A sound of martial music, light and popular. A* BOY DRUMMER *enters, drumming and goes out, followed by* LEAR, REGAN *and* GONERIL. *The music fades.* KENT *appears, behind* CLARISSA. *He is still.*)

Dear friend, it must be you. And thinking, as usual, how excellent my nature is. (*She shakes her head ruefully.*) At least you are not dead, and anything else is tolerable.

KENT: No one ever gave me a greater compliment.

CLARISSA: No?

KENT: You are truth itself and never need embellishment.

CLARISSA: I bask in your respect but don't make my life more painful.

KENT: How could I do that?

CLARISSA: By showing kindness, which cracks my armour.

KENT: You need not wear armour.

CLARISSA: No? What's life without armour?

KENT: I was on a rock. I travelled to this rock on the corpse of a bad man, bloated by his gases. So there I was, a good man, saved by putrefaction. Every day he came back, on every tide, viler and viler to behold. And then one day, he did not.

CLARISSA: He sank?

KENT: Inevitably, he sank. (*She senses his movement.*)

CLARISSA: **Do not undress.** (*Pause*)

KENT: I entertained such thoughts of you, which if I described, would make you shrink. These thoughts absorbed whole days, and kept me sane, though they were insane thoughts.

CLARISSA: How? Love's kindness.

KENT: Love's not, love never was, and if I'm vile you also are responsible — (*She goes to move.*) **Don't turn like that your hip**

CLARISSA (*amazed*): What —

KENT: **Your hip** —

CLARISSA (*horrified*): What —

KENT: **Does such** —

CLARISSA: I cannot help my hip — (KENT *covers his eyes.*) I must have caused this and forgive me, or how could you be so bad? (*He lets his hands fall.*) Your eyes are narrow with a cruelty that distorts your normally kind features, dear friend ... (*Pause. He shakes his head laughing.*)

KENT: Oh, words, oh, words kill words ...! (LEAR *returns. He looks at them.*)

LEAR: I spend whole days with Gloucester. He shows me the other kingdom. **You think there is one kingdom only**? Under the kingdom, the kingdom ...

KENT (*going to him*): Take your wife, and love her.

LEAR: Why, don't you?

KENT: Yes!

LEAR: Then she's over-loved, because you love her and I am occasionally kind, which is more than most get.

KENT: I love and suffer her.

LEAR: Good! Now have a picnic on the hill! Take some poems and a rug.

KENT: You ought not to ...!

LEAR: She reads classics — in translation — at least, the minor works —

KENT: **ought not to**.

LEAR: And sings a bit to the guitar, a sort of wail she learned in adolescent solitude —

KENT: **Ought not to piss on innocence**. (LEAR *stares at* KENT.)

LEAR: What word is that? I'm nearly stupid now, what is that? (THE DAUGHTERS *enter. They are impatient*.)

GONERIL/REGAN: Our picnic with our mum and dad!

LEAR: Not me! I have a headache!'

GONERIL/REGAN: **Oh, not another headache!**

LEAR: Yes!

CLARISSA: Yes, we need some air!

LEAR: Indeed, take Kent! (*A pause*)

CLARISSA: I think it's better if we three —

LEAR: Yes, and take Kent!

CLARISSA: The three of us merely —

LEAR: In case of wolves.

GONERIL/REGAN (*disbelief*): **Wolves?**

LEAR: Cats, then.

GONERIL/REGAN: **What cats?**

LEAR: Angry ones who once were petted. You know, or hawks with debts to settle. (*He smiles*.) Do. I hate to think of danger from the wild. (*Pause. They go out.* KENT *following.* LEAR *is left alone*.)

THE GAOL: **Lear ...!**
　　　　　　　Oh, Lear ...!
　　　　　　　May we disturb you?
　　　　　　　So many problems but we have suffered beyond
　　　　　　　Measured.

LEAR (*kneeling to them*): You say this often, as if pain had measure.

THE GAOL: **We harp on justice here**
　　　　　　　Until the word
　　　　　　　Eats tunnels through our brains

LEAR: The word's abolished, then, since it grieves so many.
　　　It must be cut out of the dictionary. **Scissors!**

THE GAOL: **Oh, Lear**
　　　　　　　You were so much kinder as a boy!

LEAR: Yes, but he was so intelligent, that boy. And he knew philosophy.

THE GAOL: **What is philosophy unless it dissolves pain?** (LEAR *sits, contemplatively, among them*.)

LEAR: Surely, it is melancholy ... be assured, I think of you often ... and need you ... oh, how I need you ... (*He gets up. The picnic party returns. They look at* LEAR. KENT *flings himself to* LEAR's *feet.*)

KENT: Execute me, then! (GONERIL *and* REGAN *go to* LEAR.)

GONERIL/REGAN: We found these flowers! Leaving them with poems, we found you flowers!

KENT: Execute me, then!

GONERIL: Execute you?

REGAN: Why is he so silly?

GONERIL/REGAN: **Execute yourself!** (*Pause.* LEAR *runs his fingers through* KENT's *hair, absently. The* DAUGHTERS *drape* LEAR *with the wild flowers, and skip off.*)

LEAR: When people loved me — and many have — I felt burdened. When they ceased to love me — I felt cold ...

CLARISSA: I can't talk of love because I know so little of it. So I'll talk of necessity instead. And how — through so much — silence — I have longed to be clamoured for. And even how, perhaps, whoever clamoured would have earned my — **You are smiling and I am trying to be honest.** (*Pause*) I am pregnant without question, and not by you. (*Pause*) Oh, listen, I had a bird once but the bird died! (*Music. The* DRUMMER *appears again, crossing the stage. They watch him pass.*)

LEAR: What is he ...!
    Hey!
    What is he ...!

Pause. He runs out. A wind and light change. LEAR *enters edging a barrel painfully onto the stage. The barrel is massive. He steadies it, stops. A newborn child is heard.* GLOUCESTER *enters holding a bundle.* LEAR *looks at him over the rim.*

LEAR: Gin.

GLOUCESTER: Bastard. (*Pause.* LEAR *lifts the lid.*)

LEAR: Love ...! (GLOUCESTER *comes slowly to the barrel. He holds the bundle out, then drops it in.* LEAR *replaces the lid.*)

GLOUCESTER: Cordelia, she calls it.

LEAR: Thank her. I have seen it, say. And add, Lear was not more arbitrary than rain. Or earthquakes. Or weapons badly aimed. (GLOUCESTER *turns to go.*) **We crawl on the earth like worms**. (*He stops.*) But she knows that. Leave the last line out. (*He goes.* KENT *enters, bows.*)

KENT: The Emperor of Endlessly Expanding Territory. (*He bows as a* DIGNITARY *enters, robed. Pause.*)

LEAR: I greet my visitors in casual dress, which is a compliment, given my inclination to be naked. (*The* EMPEROR *looks. Pause.*) I have no throne but this and you must be happy with a stool, or did you bring your own? (*He hops onto the top of the barrel and sits.* KENT *extends a stool to the* EMPEROR.) They report you very wise, which I was as a child and now am merely arbitrary. The difference is of no significance, the people will substantiate. (*Pause*) What do you want? (*Pause*)

E OF EET: There are not enough bodies in the world. (*A pause of gathering comprehension.*)

LEAR: My wife sleeps with another man. I do not love my wife. What then, is the cause of my anxiety? (*He hops off the barrel, leans on it thoughtfully. A sound of tapping from within.*) My wife will tell me everything because she cannot lie. Her inability to lie is agony to me. If she were a liar I could tolerate her. I might love a liar. If she fucked secretly in cellars with bald men I'd applaud her. I cannot help the feeling her honesty is an attempt on my sanity. (*Pause*) What do you mean, not enough bodies?

E OF EET: For the faith. (*Pause*)

LEAR: What faith?

E OF EET: There is only one faith. (*He looks into* LEAR.) Are you not tired from walking in the dark?

LEAR: Yes.

E OF EET: Are you not weary knowing all you know is false?

LEAR: Weary beyond imagination, yes.

E OF EET: And do you not ache for the solution?

LEAR: The solution's death. (*Tapping on the inside of the barrel.*)

E OF EET: But after death? (LEAR *stares.*)

LEAR: **Hor-bling!**

　　　Oh, be careful, you will explode my skull and send the splinters in your eyes!

　　　Hor-bling! (HORBLING *enters, springing as best he can and shaking a bell.*)

HORBLING: I'm getting better!

LEAR (*to the* EMPEROR): They say you executed seven hundred in an afternoon, I don't criticize, they say you blind adulterers, I don't criticize!

HORBLING: Better, but still not good! (*He skips.*)

LEAR: **He talks of after death**. (*He stares at* HORBLING. *Sounds from inside the barrel.* HORBLING *hears it, amazed.*)

E OF EET: I come to you, when being the greatest power in the world, it was more fitting you should come to me. But I have no pride. I never conquer. I only deliver. (HORBLING *scrambles to the side of the barrel, listens.*)

LEAR (*still reeling*): **After — death**? (REGAN *and* GONERIL *enter.*)

GONERIL/REGAN: Our mother says the baby where is it?

LEAR: This man says there are not enough bodies for the faith. This man has seven million soldiers on the frontiers.

GONERIL/REGAN: Cordelia, she says, where is she?

LEAR: **Seven million unafraid of death!** (*The* DAUGHTERS *look at the* EMPEROR.)

REGAN: Stab him.

GONERIL: Hang him up by his heels.

LEAR (*to the* EMPEROR): Children! Aren't they miraculous? Do you have children? **I've thought of that**.

GONERIL: He would look different naked. Where's the baby, our mother says.

HORBLING (*flinging himself at the* EMPEROR'*s feet*): Seven million? (*He point to* LEAR.) There is the enemy of the faith! There is cynicism and apostasy! (*He drags off his cap and takes out the now decaying papers*.) This plan requires five years to change the kingdom from a lair of beasts to Paradise! Five years, and I revise it frequently, these corrections are illegible I will admit, no — the wrong way up — here — no, that's smudged, it says — I translate — do you have a minute, I — that's the introduction, skip that — it's — this page goes there — (*He falters as* CLARISSA *enters. Pause*.)

LEAR: She does not put on lipstick, Clarissa. Or any false thing. (*Pause*)

CLARISSA: Where is my baby?

GONERIL/REGAN: We asked and he —

CLARISSA: Cordelia? (LEAR *chooses to be silent, walking a line in silence, and returning to the spot, thoughtfully.* CLARISSA *lets out a mournful cry. She falls to her knees and beats the ground with her fists*.)

CLARISSA: **I've done nothing! I've done nothing**! (*She stops. She straightens herself*.)

LEAR (*to the* EMPEROR): Do you do dinners? That is what is wanted here. (*The* EMPEROR *stares at him*.) I loved a woman. She made death possible, and yet to die would be to lose her, therefore she kept me living ... (*Pause*) Bring you armies. And I'll be burned. Or skinned. Or whatever it is you do. (*Suddenly, as if on an impulse,* LEAR *rushes to the barrel and flings off the lid, which rolls. He plunges in his arms and pulls out the dripping bundle of* CORDELIA.)

 Gin!

 Gin!

 And she still lives! (*He holds it up, smothers it with kisses*.)

 Oh, was that good?

 Oh, was that a good thing, hey? (*The* EMPEROR, *in disbelief, rises to his feet. The baby cries*.)

GONERIL/REGAN (*jumping up and down*): **Oh, Oh, our sis-ter! Oh, Oh, our sis-ter**! (LEAR *thrusts the dripping baby at the girls, and kneeling at the* EMPEROR'*s feet, tears open his collar to expose his throat*.)

LEAR: Seven million daggers.

 Seven million knives! (*The* EMPEROR *stares*.)

CLARISSA (*to the* EMPEROR): You see how terrible we find life? How it maddens us? Don't offer us another ... (*Pause. The* EMPEROR *places a hand on her, in a gesture of profound pity.* HORBLING *tears up his five-year plan, gazing on* LEAR, *and withdraws. The light changes, the* EMPEROR *goes out.* LEAR *remains in the posture*.)

LEAR: I wanted to die. And you saved me. I was ready to die. **The**

third time you have saved me! (*He stares at* CLARISSA *in horror. A second light change.* CORDELIA *enters.*)

CORDELIA: I think if he had drowned me, I should have forgiven him . . .!

KENT (*entering*): You are at an age when the agonized seem beautiful. Yet there are thousands curse him every day.

CORDELIA: I call them vermin for it!

KENT: I am not trying to make you hate your father, merely — (*He shrugs.*)

CORDELIA (*to* KENT): I do think, when you speak, it is as if each word had weights attached to it which catch your teeth. You are utterly kind to me but. Perhaps you harbour some sex thing for me, in which case I wish you'd say — (KENT *seethes.*) Is that wrong? I'm often wrong. I get that from my father, not from my mother, who is never wrong and can't be, it seems.

CLARISSA (*extending her hands as if conducting a walk*): **Chil-dren!**

CORDELIA: But if it is so, I wish you would admit it. A thought is better born that smothered, **there now I sound like her!** (*She grins.*)

KENT: **Nothing of the sort.** (*Pause*)

CLARISSA (*enters*): **Chil-dren!**

CORDELIA: Oh, good. (*She smiles.*) Oh, good! (REGAN *and* GONERIL *hurry in.*)

GONERIL/REGAN: We're going to a dance.

CLARISSA: Later.

GONERIL/REGAN: Going to a dance and now we're late! (*They stare at* CLARISSA. LEAR *is motionless.*)

CLARISSA: I must show you something I have found. (*The sound of the* GAOL CHORUS.)

THE GAOL: **Where's Lear?**
           No one comes here but Lear
           You hurt our eyes with strangeness!

GONERIL/REGAN/CORDELIA: Let's play houses! Let's fly kites! **Let's build castles on the beach!**

CLARISSA: Hold hands, I said!

THE GAOL: **He does not licence visitors!** (*Pause.* LEAR *at last abandons his posture, and rising, comes to them.*)

LEAR: You have found the one place I can discover sanity . . .

CLARISSA: Free them.

LEAR: You have trespassed in my garden . . . (*Pause*)

CLARISSA: Garden . . .? (*Pause. With infinite slowness, a chain swings twice, like a pendulum, between them. A wind.*)
           Free them. Lear.
           Free them.

THE GAOL: **Our suffering is over**
           Our bodies are returned to us
           Do you remember how it felt to own your body?

They laugh madly, uncontrollably, and stop

LEAR: I said to the inmates of the gaol, when I have done a crime sufficient to dwarf not only what you did, but what you have imagined, then daylight's yours. The gaoled are only in the gaol by being worse than their gaolers. How else? (*Pause. The chain swings again and stops.*) **Oh, who will correct me when my wife is gone ?**

CORDELIA: I will ... (REGAN *and* GONERIL *look at each other with profound realisation.*)

GONERIL/REGAN: Let's go to the dance!

CORDELIA (*releasing the hand of* CLARISSA): How hard it is to say this, but I do not pity you. I think you never did a bad thing in your life. Or let a false emotion slip through your net. Or postured. Or ever were corrupt. And I think — shall I go on?

GONERIL/REGAN: Do go on!

CORDELIA: I have a deep and until today, an unstirred hatred for you. (*The chain swings again.*)

GONERIL/REGAN: **It's true! It's true! She does say things which we find impossible to express**! (*Pause*)

CLARISSA: Don't hurt me. Someone must do good. And of all people I've done least to — (*Pause. She breaks into a sobbing laugh.*) What's that to do with anything! (*Pause*) I've never exaggerated. And I am not going to now.

CORDELIA: **Do! Oh, Do exaggerate** ...! (CLARISSA *shakes her head defiantly. The chain passes again. A cacophony breaks in.*)

ALL: **Mummy/Daddy/where are my/going to a dance I said/have you seen my/comb your hair you look/Daddy/shoes and socks/Christmas is so/we love each other don't we/Mummy/love each other so/and holidays are/will you stop quarrelling/and my Dad says/I said stop that/I said/I said/get out the photographs**! (*It stops. The chain again, observed this time by* LEAR.)

LEAR: God wants her for the comfort of His solitude ... We can't be blamed ... (*With a sudden access of energy,* LEAR *leaps and clings to the chain, usurping it.*)
> **Raise Me!**
> **Raise me then, God!**

He swings to and fro, pitiful and absurd. The light on CLARISSA *fades. After some minutes,* GLOUCESTER *appears.*

GLOUCESTER: May I have her, do you think? (*They look at him.*) I mean, there can be no particular requirement for ... When I was a beggar I made lovers of the dead since I was ... scarcely a proper suitor for the living ... (LEAR *swings.*) And they are — perfectly passionate ...

CORDELIA (*to* GLOUCESTER): Take me away. To some corner of the wood. And do whatever you do to young women. (*The* DRUMMER *is heard, and the band music.* LEAR *jumps down. The* THREE DAUGHTERS *crowd to* LEAR *and embrace him. The* DRUMMER *comes nearer.*)

LEAR: Hey! (*The* DRUMMER *enters, passing.* LEAR *chases him.*) Who are you?

DRUMMER: Happiness!

LEAR: But I never wanted happiness! Why do I follow you, therefore? (*A sudden and terrible wind. Snow fall.*)

SEVENTH LEAR

The CHORUS OF THE GAOL *lies heaped and dead.* LEAR *is sitting in overcoats on a folding stool. Through the wind* KENT *staggers on with a chess table. He places it before* LEAR *and unfolds his own stool. He sits. They study. A long time passes.* KENT *goes to make a move.*

LEAR: Erm! (KENT *stops in mid-movement. Pause. He continues to move.*)

Erm! (*He stops again.*)

If I may say so.

Begging your.

Etcetera but. (KENT *finishes the move.*)

Erm! (KENT *looks resentful.* LEAR *turns aside.*) I do think cheating is peculiar, so peculiar, because even when the cheat might win on skill alone he still prefers to cheat. It is impossible to satisfy him. I have watched you cheating for eight years.

KENT: Eight years . . .?

LEAR: Eight years to the day and never once protested.

KENT: I admit nothing. But why today?

LEAR: Why, indeed? Yes, why today? If only we were constant, if only we were! But today I felt it necessary to protest — no — not protest exactly — but to announce my knowledge of your cheating, which I had detected on the first day.

KENT: If only you had said.

LEAR: If only I had, but what difference would it have made? Do continue cheating, I merely wished to acquaint you with the fact I knew — (KENT *suddenly rises to his feet, pointing to the* CHORUS *and letting out a moan.*) Now you are trying to change the subject — (*He groans.*) I apologize for spoiling what was a perfectly innocuous and trivial practice — (*He points.*) I am pedant! I am a pedant! I admit it! (*Pause. The wind blows.* LEAR *seems shrunken in his chair.*) Please move . . .

THE GAOL: **We knew How else could we be free? But knowing How could we be allowed to live?**

LEAR: Please move . . . (KENT *looks at him, then in a spasm of love, reaches out his hand and clasps* LEAR's *across the table.*)

GOLGO
Sermons on Pain and Privilege

Golgo was first performed by The Wrestling School at the Haymarket Theatre, Leicester, on 22nd November, 1989 with the following cast:

WHATTO (m)	Roger Frost
STONEHEART (m)	Benny Young
GLORIA (f)	Jane Bertish
JANE (f)	Julie-Kate Olivier
THE PRIEST (m)	Jemma Redgrave
RUBBER (m)	Kenny Ireland
GOODGIRL (f)	Philippa Vafadari
AGNEW (m)	Philip Franks
FORGET (f)	Tricia Kelly
CHILD	
CHORUS	The Company

The Witnesses of Golgotha
PILATE
JOSEPH
MARY MAGDALENE
THE SOLDIERS
BARABBAS
THE THIEVES

The Unrecorded Witnesses of Golgotha
THE EXECUTIONER
THE LUNATIC
THE MAN WITH THE MIRROR

The parts taken by the characters:

RUBBER	Joseph
FORGET	Mary
STONEHEART	Pilate
GOODGIRL	Magdalene
AGNEW	Blind Soldier
THE PRIEST	Barabbas
AGNEW/PRIEST	The Thieves
WHATTO	The Lunatic
THE PRIEST	Man With The Mirror
RUBBER	The Executioner
WHATTO	Christ

DESIGNED BY	Simon Eliott and Brendon O'Connor
MUSIC BY	Matthew Scott
DIRECTED BY	Nicholas Le Prevost

The Setting:
A Park in France, 1789. In darkness, a hammering, which ceases.

Three crosses of inordinate height. A coat hanging by a nail. WORKMEN *in a posture of completion. They await* WHATTO. *Their hands hang by their sides.*

CHORUS **If he disgusts you**
        How right that it
        His self-advertisement
        Is incorrigible

A figure enters, and stops at the edge of the stage.

        Look, how owning everything
        He despises you

The WORKMEN *bow their heads.*

        His immoderate and wholly
        Indulgent character
        Lacking both spontaneity
        And social conscience
        Fills you with
        Implacable contempt

WHATTO *walks to the central cross and running his hands over it, embraces it.*

        I don't think
        He ever danced in his life
        Stroked a dog
        Or
        Tapped
        A
        Foot
        To
        Music

The WORKMEN *walk off. The sound of a brush scrubbing, and the clang of a bucket. A wind blows. A* WOMAN *appears, kneeling, and advancing in* WHATTO's *tracks, eradicates his footprints with water. She arrives at last where he is clinging to the cross. She stops. A small bell is heard. A procession appears, with baskets. It crosses the stage, goes off, in a cloud of volubility.*

WHATTO: This love you feel for me

This excoriating and disintegrating sickness
Please, I'm talking
This antithesis of kindness which

GLORIA: **Not love.**

WHATTO: And renders you an object of undisguised.

GLORIA: **Not Love.**

WHATTO: Contempt etcetera. Much of which spills on me.

GLORIA: **Not Love I said.**

WHATTO (*abandoning his embrace*): Not that I care. Not that humilia-
tion ever left its stain on me but. And its relentless nature. No, it
strains all pity and pity I was never gifted with. I am sorry I fucked
you, to be honest there was no beauty in it and. (*She is scrubbing
the cross where he has leaned against it.*) None at all. (*She finishes
removing his traces. He looks at her a long time. He goes to her with
swift strides and is about to plunder her skirts when the sound of a
bell is heard and the procession reappears.*) It's here! I'm here! Thank
you for passing! Thank you for returning! My hollow and arid life
I lay down as a rug, I spread as a threadbare and worm-rotted carpet.
Tread me! I long to suffocate beneath your feet! Though you are
pack of nobodies I ache to feel your heels . . . (*Pause*).

GLORIA: **He thinks love you put down like a hairbrush. Never.** (*Pause.
They stand uncomfortably. She moves the bucket. She begins to eradicate
the prints of* WHATTO's *feet. The sky is instantly overcast. The procession disposes itself with its baskets. They settle. A figure emerges
from the left. He commands their attentiveness. The sound of the scrubbing brush ceases. Pause.*)

STONEHEART: Vox Populi. (*The assembly whistles and claps. He
silences them with a gesture.*) The foul-breathed scum. Put him up
there. (*He gestures to the top of the cross.*) Not I or Rome. Not any
savage magistrate wielding the arcane law. No snob. No dinner-suited
diner pink from chandeliers. Or claque of dapper lawyers with their
whores. (*Pause*) Vox Populi put him up there. (*With calculation, he
draws a towel from under his coat. They applaud. He wipes his hands
and tosses it to them. They reach for it. He silences them again with
a gesture.*) No, it's problem, democracy.

GLORIA: **Not a Hairbrush, is it? Love?** (*Pause*)

STONEHEART: Its tendencies to pull the bowels from innocence. Its
— (*A* WOMAN *enters. He stops, seeing her. She looks only at him.*)
You said you weren't coming. How typical of you to come, having
declared you were not coming. (*Pause*).

How magnificent

Enraging

And directly from another man I see. (*Pause. She does not move or
take her eyes from him. He resumes.*)

Manic upheavals in which tolerance is ridiculed and unison proclaims
the extirpation of dissent, its breathless sloganizing, and corruption
of benighted words, its — (*She walks.*) No, you are sabotaging my
speech. (*She stops.*)

JANE: Pilate's body was more beautiful than Christ's. Its stoop. Its hanging hands of passivity. Could you love a triumphant man? I never could.

WHATTO: **He is haranguing, let him harangue, will you?**

JANE: Yes.

WHATTO (*going to her*): No, it is magnificent to see you, to witness you, beautiful, and we shall soon be dead, we shall be diced, who am I to criticize, who never loved life from the beginning, who was born to enjoy nothing and to see the horror even in a kiss, no, you are wearing wonderful things and if I were capable of admiration I should certainly admire you, do sit, or stand if you prefer it, we cannot tear our eyes from you and my outburst was unforgivable, try to remember my better qualities, do you want a chair? (GLORIA *has followed in* WHATTO's *tracks, washing them out.*)

STONEHEART: She fucks on afternoons like this.

WHATTO: Of course she does, and with men of no distinction. Yes, that is lovely material, today you can buy anything, there is much to be said for today! I think as I am dying, as I am diced, I shall think, there was at least this one thing to be said for today, its plenitude! Is it taffeta or what, I am so ignorant of fabrics.

JANE: Silk.

WHATTO (*to* STONEHEART): Are you continuing, I love your diatribe, I also hate democracy but you know more about it!

CHORUS: **Is he not repulsive?**
Would you care if he died?
He has done things of such barbarity
His manner is an alibi

GLORIA *follows* WHATTO *with the bucket.*

And we who know a thing or two about depravity
Say wit is unmistakably
The fashion of the cruel.

STONEHEART (*who has been staring at* JANE): How did he, then? Or was it several? I am seventy and now my speech has gone, I am the minister for finances and she. On the grass or in a room? And there is a bite on your neck. Oh, that is coarse, that is the very stamp of low loving, I must apologize, the speech is everywhere now, look, she has democracy upon her neck, she flows with it and I. (*Pause.* WHATTO *goes to* STONEHEART *and embraces him.*)

WHATTO: Thank you for coming. (*He looks into his eyes. A wind. The* COMPANY *leans, in unison, but for* WHATTO *and* GLORIA.)

GLORIA: I love you and you must pay the price.

WHATTO: There is a price, is there?

GLORIA: Yes.

WHATTO: What price? All my life I slipped by without paying.

GLORIA: I will haunt you till you die. And as you lie in bed, I shall not wipe your mouth, but beat the pans and drop the crockery.

WHATTO: I made a mistake with you.

GLORIA: Your cries for water will go unheeded.

WHATTO: Yes.

GLORIA: And all the dealers I will invite to haggle for the furniture.

WHATTO: I can hear them.

GLORIA: The crash of wardrobes past your dying door.

WHATTO: Yes, well, you have all the vision of the compulsively compassionate but I shan't die in bed, I am to be diced, I am to be the single focus of a popular hatred, hunted, trapped, devoured, **Whatto was there and then he wasn't**. It is amazing the speed with which a mob consumes a piece of flesh. Once man. Once thinking. Once loved. (*She stares at him.*)

GLORIA: I think if you took me in your arms now, I should turn coke, I should turn concrete . . . (*The wind ceases. The figure of* JOSEPH *rises from the assembly. He goes with infinite slowness to the foot of the cross, and looks up.*)

JOSEPH: Not too late, I hope? (*Pause*) Son? (*Pause. His hands hang.*) Oh, but it's been a **most knotted life**, mine. (*Pause. He looks to the others.*) I don't think he remembers me. (*They laugh.*)

Well, who am I, indeed? Another nobody in the unravelling ribbon of indifference, or is that wrong? You tell me. (*Pause*) But here I am, and spare us a minute from superior thought. (*Pause*) It's **not-your-dad**, come to see **not-my-son**. (*The assembly laughs.*) You know, the one who walked around like misery and taught you tenon joints — (*They laugh.*) Shut up, shut up — (*He shakes his head.*) How far I've come to be with you, I tell you things were driven through my palms also. (*They laugh. He rebukes.*) Yes, that's pain, too! (*He addresses the cross.*) They laugh at me! How they detest the failure, how it detests the failure! And I am, I am, admittedly. I'm not too late, am I? Fifty miles is a stroll for a bloke my age, and I was never young, never, never young, which must explain a great deal of her. Well, I couldn't stick the discos and she. Your mother. Only seventeen when we.

MARY (*rising to her feet*): Why have you turned up in the name of. Why, for God's sake?

JOSEPH: I don't know. Why have I?

MARY: And come here moaning when he. Staggering about and bleating. Always you bleated.

JOSEPH: Did I?

MARY: Why wreck a death with your old protests?

JOSEPH: I don't know. I do not know. Yes, I do.

MARY: I thought you were bedridden.

JOSEPH: I was. Give us the chair.

MARY: No.

JOSEPH: He's very still. Give us a sandwich.

MARY: No. (*The assembly claps.*)

JOSEPH: Still as if asleep but he knows who I am, **you know all right**. He did well, didn't he, but the well-doers are always on the backs of others not so celebrated. Me, for one. I don't complain. Me, for one. **Things were driven through my palms also**. (*The assembly boos* JOSEPH.) All right, all right, but that's pain also! Give us the chair.

MARY: No.

JOSEPH: I found the strength to move, but was it hate? I got out of my sickbed **without a miracle**. (*They boo again*.) No miracle, the sick man moved by hate. It lasts, you see, it does last, hate. (*They hiss*.) **You sit there, what do you know about paternity?** Give us a sandwich.

MARY: No.

JOSEPH: Miracles for everyone. What about me? If anyone required a miracle it was me, **Not-The-Dad** of **Not-The-Son!** (*He laughs, shaking his head.*)

MARY: Go home, and I'll cook for you again. I can't say more than that, can I? Cook and change the linen. (*He shakes his head.*)

JOSEPH: Don't want to be cooked for, and utterly unafraid of death ... (*He looks at* MARY.) And she was pretty ... (*The assembly boos.*) Yes! Pretty, she was! **Oh, Memory, the knife of it! Oh, Memory, its razor kick!** (*Pause. The sky darkens.* MARY *brings him a chair, in which he sits, sunken. It rains. The assembly puts up umbrellas.* WHATTO *places his own hat on* JOSEPH's *bare head, and letting out a cry, tears open his shirt to expose it to the weather.*)

WHATTO: **Whatto! Music And Infinite Triviality!**

STONEHEART: Though I adore the ivory tower, on some days I come down into the crowd. Though the ivory tower is so dangerous, some days I seek the relief of the gutter, which is safe. You must know, after all, what everybody knows. At least sometimes. At least a little of. And I am a minister. So it behoves me. A little of.

WHATTO (*as the sun appears*):

> **My**
> **Friends**
> **Oh**
> **They**
> **Flock**
> **They**
> **Cluster**
> **Their**
> **Adoration**
> **Soddens**
> **Me!** (*He strolls among them.*)

Oh, what is it you love, do say! Oh, try to put into words what compels you to pester me! Am I a drug, am I a narcotic? Am I, once tasted, impossible to forget? **Don't all speak at once!** Is it my depth? Is it my unfathomable mystery? I am a well in a wood, whose mossy sides plunge down to cool and bottomless sweet waters, **who has the courage to swim my soul**? (*They take down their umbrellas.* GOODGIRL *Gets up, smoothing her frock.*)

GOODGIRL: I'll make my contribution. Shall I? I'll make my contribution. All night I sat with pen and paper and then I threw it all away. Why, did you say? Because everything I do is inferior to my conviction that I might do things of excellence. Yes, excellence. My tutor says what's excellence, it's only relative, do not be intimidated by this thing, how thin you are through fretting about excellence, you grind your bones to power. **It exists however it exists.** (*Pause. She is quite still.*) But obviously, the odds are very much against me. I almost certainly will fail. (*Pause. She collects her powers.*)
Magdalen. (*The assembly whistles and louts.*)
Why not I've got sex too, why not! I have and
She (*They bawl.*)
Yes
You
I've been
I've
Suffered the
Yes
You bastards
Yes (*They stop, in a bawl of laughter. She prepares an entrance. Suddenly the* PRIEST *stands up.*)
PRIEST (*with a single bell*): Complexity is a conspiracy against the people! (*He dings again.*)
They have nothing to learn they do not know already! (*And again.*)
Go among them for they possess the key!
GOODGIRL (*turning on him viciously*): **To what! To what! The key to what!** (*Silence. The* PRIEST *freezes.* GOODGIRL *recovers.*) Magdalene. (*She makes her entrance.*)
MARY: You came, then. And I said, she will be late as always. Didn't I?
JOSEPH: Give her a chance.
MARY: Late and a bit slovenly.
JOSEPH: Give the girl a chance, I said.
MAGDALENE: Already I feel his words are fading with his breath.
MARY: Hear that?
JOSEPH: She's only human, fuck it . . .!
MARY (*to* JOSEPH): **You are too forgiving! Always, too forgiving!** One thing I could not stick in you, one thing above all others, this comprehensive spirit of forgiveness, especially towards whores, oddly. (JOSEPH *groans.*) You groan, especially towards whores! (*She turns to* MAGDALENE.) That is a lovely dress, even if your breasts hang out — (JOSEPH *groans.* MARY *slaps him. He shakes his head, with resignation.* MARY *takes* MAGDALENE *in her arms with a spontaneous embrace.*) Listen, listen, I am the mother, a vixen or a bitch for my son, do you blame me?
MAGDALENE: No.
MARY: Kiss me, then. You are the cow of cows if you return to whoring after all he did for you.

MAGDALENE: Already I feel his words are fading with his breath.

MARY: Listen, your breasts are your worst enemies, your mouth's a crab on your face and your arse will murder you!

MAGDALENE: Yes ...

MARY: And he had no criticism of you! Never! None! (*Pause.* MAGDALENE *moves, stops.*)

MAGDALENE: I want to be touched. (*The assembly hoots.* GOODGIRL *stamps.*) **Shut Up!**

PRIEST (*dinging the bell*): Go to the People! There is the truth! (*He dings again.*) Knowledge lies on the lips of the poor! (*He dings again, but before he can speak,* JANE *seizes the bell from him and flings it offstage, where it tinkles pitifully. Pause.*)

MAGDALENE: Not all were vile, you see. But some came seeking, I don't know what. Some came to murder, but some came differently. Some touched me tenderly, and wordless, and others were verbose, while others, seeming to study me, were overcome with anger. What this was, I never understood. Nor could he ever tell me what it was they sought. I wish to be touched. I have to be touched. To be touched. I have to be touched. (*She lowers her head for some seconds, then lifts it with exhilaration.*) Excellence! Excellence, surely!

WHATTO: Listen! (*The distant sounds of music and a crowd. They crane their necks. A long pause.*) How near they are ... how near and gathering ... (*The sounds fade.* GOODGIRL *sits with the assembly, and puts her arms round* AGNEW, *laughing with relief. They chatter wildly.*)

JOSEPH: She wasn't like that ...

WHATTO: What does it matter?

JOSEPH: It doesn't matter, but she wasn't like that ...

WHATTO: **What are you, a literalist? What are you, an archivist?**

JOSEPH: Not at all, but —

WHATTO: **What are you a taxidermist?**

JOSEPH: No, I —

WHATTO: Forgive me, I am cruel today, forgive me I am so far from my intention, I am so grateful to you but who would know, the way I treat you, who would guess my gratitude?

JOSEPH: Well, I don't know —

WHATTO: No one would know! Forgive me! I shall be so apologetic you will squirm, you will suffer the embarrassment of one who witnesses the decline of once-great characters, am I forgiven?

JOSEPH: Obviously, I only meant —

WHATTO (*ignoring him, turning to the rest*): **One of the soldiers was blind!**

AGNEW: Me!

WHATTO: Yes! And sings!

AGNEW: Me also! (*He jumps to his feet, clears his throat. The assembly claps.*)

GLORIA (*to* WHATTO): It is not a tap, love, is it? **It's not a tap!** (*she drags the bucket behind* WHATTO.)

BLIND SOLDIER (*closing his eyes and singing*):

I am in love with a yellow-skinned woman,
Whose arse is cool as ice,
She will bury me one day and weeping for less
than an hour,
Sell my tunic! (*He moves, groping.*)

I am in love with a white-haired woman,
Whose teeth are rotting.
She abuses me as illiterate and worthless
cannon-fodder then laughing,
Licks my body! (*He moves nearer the cross.*)

I am in love with a stooping woman,
Whose lip is cracked and dry,
She teaches me to repeat political slogans
whose meaning defeats me,
Then fucks my brother! (*They cheer him. He stumbles.*)

STONEHEART (*to* JANE): Today I am seventy.

JANE: I know. My love. And I did not send you flowers, knowing
the neglect would lash you. My love. I knew your spy would say,
today she had a single visitor . . .

BLIND SOLDIER (*under the cross and staring up*): **I'm blind** . . .! (*Pause.
Silence.*) I thought I'd mention it.

THIN SOLDIER: Why not . . .?

BLIND SOLDIER: In this particular place. At this particular moment.
Since —

THIN SOLDIER: Why not, indeed?

BLIND SOLDIER: I didn't want to thrust myself, but time is passing
and —

THIN SOLDIER: Say it again, he didn't hear you.

BLIND SOLDIER: **I'm blind!** (*Silence*)
                            Horribly blind! (*Pause*)
               No, I exaggerate. All blindness is. So why pile on
the.

THIN SOLDIER: No, pile it on, we won't will we? We won't criticize.
You have to make the case, obviously.

BLIND SOLDIER (*wailing now*): **Blind** . . .! (*Silence*)
Is he dead, or what?

THIN SOLDIER: Far from it.

BLIND SOLDIER: **Time for one more miracle, surely?** (*Pause*) Or
not? (*Pause. He leans his hands on the cross. After a few moments,
he shakes his head pitifully.*) Still blind . . . (*He turns away from the
cross, stops.*) Funny. I never complained about blindness. I was born
blind and I never did complain until. I never did, you know that,
John.

THIN SOLDIER: It's true.

BLIND SOLDIER: And now — for the first time in my life — I feel my blindness is a burden.

THIN SOLDIER: It hardly is in your case, you are so —

BLIND SOLDIER: Yes, I am so deft —

THIN SOLDIER: So deft you never thought this bloke is blind —

BLIND SOLDIER: Never, but now — (*He trips.*) **Fuck, I stumbled!** (*In horror he clasps his face. The assembly gives him some seconds, then applauds wildly.*)

WHATTO: I loved that! I so loved that! Oh, the excellence of that and I do not like the man, I do not like Agnew, forgive me if I am honest, I have never liked dentists, especially dentists who are communists, them I like least! Why are you not rioting? Why are you not speaking from a barricade? (AGNEW *shrugs.*) No, it is bad faith with you! You love my company no matter what is happening on the barricades, **Or. Or. Or.** (*He commands silence with a raised finger.*) You are only here as an adieu. And walking from my garden, you will make towards the sounds of dissolution, discarding your wig, and draping garments on the trees ... (AGNEW *shrugs.*) Put your glasses on. (AGNEW *does so.*) Yes .... Oh, the prosecutor **and I shall cheat you I shall deprive you I shall** Oh, the prosecutor, **I shall evade the consequences of!**

GOODGIRL (*stroking* AGNEW's *hair*): He is not like that!

WHATTO: **No, and nor was I!** (*Pause. He smiles.*)
  Nor was I ... (*He crouches by* AGNEW.)
  He longs for learning. He does not know yet the consequence of learning. To him it seems a door. And all doors must be opened.

GLORIA: You should know.

WHATTO: If only because —

GLORIA: You should know.

WHATTO: They're doors.

GLORIA: **You should know I said**. (*Pause*)

WHATTO: I do. (*Pause*) Consequently, the greatest power lies with him who can say of the door, oh, you are a door, and you have hinges. Oh, you are open, you are an aperture in the wall.

GLORIA: **He knows all about apertures**!

WHATTO (*rising in frustration*): **I am trying to save this youth!** (*Pause*) She's right. Her criticism — if you can call that criticism — is perfectly right. (*He walks away, distracted.*)

GLORIA: All he says. Believe it. All he says. Is true. (*Pause. A sound. She begins to scrub.*)

CHORUS: **We warn you**
  It must be time to warn you
  Of this way he has

  Look at him standing
  You might almost think him sensitive
  Yes It's time to warn you
  Of this way he has

Before you know it
He'll twist your horror into pity
DON'T

The enemies of ordinary people
THAT'S YOU AND ME
Are so skilled at pretending
Their pain is complicated
By their privilege
DON'T

We trust you to discriminate
Between the manipulators
And the genuinely contrite
DON'T

STONEHEART: I can continue —
CHORUS: **DON'T**
STONEHEART: I can continue I suppose because all pain like water on the sand goes. Like papers on the wind go, I'll continue —
WHATTO: I think we want the thieves now. Don't we? (*Pause*) There is going to be such bloodshed. And in this bloodshed I will die. And one of you, in protecting me from the fury of the mob, will also die. And I quite like the mob! Unlike you, I like it! Its dogs. Its mangey and unmuzzled. Its swallowing of lunatic and baby-blinding substances. I love its barmy colours and the way its arse hangs out. (*Pause*)
JANE (*of* STONEHEART): This man alone knows how to be intimate. And it's a fact that few want intimacy, for the reason that few want privacy. And they are the same. I mean, if we were forever being handled how could we demonstrate love? Who here, for example, really wants intimacy?
AGNEW: Me!
GOODGIRL: Me!
JANE: No, that's warmth you're after.
AGNEW: Yes, warmth, but —
JANE: That's the pig at the teat. I don't mean that.
RUBBER: Don't call him a pig at a —
JANE: It's nothing to do with warmth, I said. (*She goes to* STONE-HEART.) This man knows how hard it is. How much labour goes into intimacy. How much coldness and calculation goes into an act of love. And he is old.
STONEHEART: Old and washed. Old and fragrant.
JANE: Yes! How I shall miss you!
STONEHEART: And that missing will be the greatest intimacy yet. My dear. My true and unashamed one. (*She kisses him. The* TWO THIEVES *leap up and rush to their crosses, crying abuse.*)

THE THIEVES: **Hey, you**
Oh, curse your pisslife you
Oh, fuck your
And we dying
How we roar your envy and
Spray our spit!

WHATTO *laughs as* THE THIEVES, *in torment and fury, spit on the unmoving couple, roaring. Their languorous kiss is undisturbed. With a sudden gesture,* GLORIA *throws her bucket of water over the lovers. Still they are unmoved. Silence ensues. The water drips off them.* GOOD-GIRL *gets up, and goes near to them, as if to a curiosity. She lets out a sob. Her shoulders heave.* GLORIA *drops the bucket with a clutter.*)

GLORIA: Should I have done that? I don't know.

GOODGIRL: I also have a life . . . ! I also have a life . . . !

PRIEST: Pay not attention to acts of love whose individualism is out of keeping with the times! Can I have my bell, please? Ignore all manifestations of corruption which in an age of equality are simply comic! Where's my bell? The people love and their love is manifest in children. Note these have no progeny! I'd like the bell, whoever threw it, please . . . (WHATTO *goes to the* PRIEST.)

WHATTO: I think, when you die, it will be the worst. I think, for you, the very worst must be imagined.

PRIEST: Yes. (WHATTO *looks at him, holding his hand. Suddenly he turns to* THE THIEVES.)

WHATTO: Time rushes on! And we, who got the time wrong, have less than anybody! Give us the thieves! I love the thieves, the thieves are after all a class, the thieves are the sole and eternal spirit of democracy and they so rarely speak! They so rarely articulate their complex motivations!

THE THIEVES: **We wish we'd never done it**.

WHATTO: Obviously, but you can do better than that!

THE THIEVES: **We wouldn't have done it if we'd known!**

WHATTO: Please, I am sophisticated! And my friends are waiting their turn! (*They look, dumbly.*) That's it, is it? (*Pause*) I invite you here, at a critical juncture in human history, **I assure you it is a critical juncture whether you recognize it or not**, I invite you to elaborate the ecstasy of theft, **Do you expect them to announce themselves, these junctures**, and you are silent, silent as the rock pool at low tide . . . (GLORIA *enters with a new bucket of water. She puts it down.*) No, you must exert yourselves. You must leap the obvious, I beg you . . . (STONEHEART *and* JANE *separate.*)

FIRST THIEF: Thank you. (*They are unsteady. They part without looking at one another.*) Thank you because the dying are consumed with envy . . .

SECOND THIEF: Not me . . .

FIRST THIEF: Not you, but I am, she is a rag, look, love has made a rag of her . . .

SECOND THIEF: I had women . . .
FIRST THIEF: Yes . . .
SECOND THIEF: How they loved me . . .!
FIRST THIEF: Is that so . . .?
SECOND THIEF: Thieve me, they said. The married ones especially. Thieve me!
FIRST THIEF (*look after her*): She is all pain, she is all absence . . .
SECOND THIEF: Plunder me by night, they said, all my locks are broken . . . (*The* FIRST THIEF *sings.*)
FIRST THIEF: Show me your belly!

> I'd suffer this twice to witness it!
> I'd given Heaven to the undeserving rich
> And the violent could use
> Paradise as a football pitch
> For your belly showing!
>
> Show me your arse!
> I'd be dragged over glass to see it hanging!
> I'd starve the unborn of the whole universe
> And the poor could endure a pain even worse than poverty
> For your arse showing!
>
> Show me your breasts!
> I'd lie under armies to see them swinging!
> I'd tread in the mouth of a brief-stricken mother
> And the bodies of children could smother my little pity
> For your breasts showing!
>
> Show me your cunt!
> I'd be torn by dogs to see all its colours!
> I'd tell God
> He can keep his right hand,
> My corpse can be kicked under the sand of Israel
> For your cunt showing!

> *Pause*

SECOND THIEF: She won't, however, will she? For a thief? (*Pause*)
STONEHEART: Show him.
SECOND THIEF: **Don't be a party to their
                          Don't be an item of their**
STONEHEART: Show him.
SECOND THIEF: **Don't be a thing in their fucklife!**
FIRST THIEF: Why not? If she. Why not! (*Pause.* JANE *walks to the foot of his cross.*) It's not for me, is it? (*She shakes her head.*) It isn't pity? (*She shakes her head.*) Which I, in any case, have never really understood.
SECOND THIEF: **They're stealing your death for their bedroom!** (*Pause*)

I say no more.
I say no more.
I'm silent.

Pause. JANE *undoes her dress by the front, button by button. When it is done, she looks resolutely at* STONEHEART. *The lights have dimmed to evening. Pause, then a burst of enthusiastic applause from the assembly.*

WHATTO: Oh, what you can do if you try!

GLORIA: It's not an overcoat, love, is it? **It's not an overcoat!**

WHATTO: **I don't know what it is! Ask them!** (*He embraces* RUBBER.) I so liked that! I so appreciated the audacity of that, whilst thinking audacity is not everything, it is nevertheless the condition of every-thing! **I was audacious but perhaps not audacious enough!** There is the problem! I am a failure of such staggering proportions but at least I have examined it, at least I look my failure in the eye! For that I deserve some sympathy. Perhaps a little more audacity was all that was required, but it's too late now, **Or is it**? (*He takes the* PRIEST *by the shoulders.*) Who are you?

PRIEST: The actor.

WHATTO: What actor? The actor, he says! There was no actor!

PRIEST: Barabbas was an actor.

WHATTO: Is that so? I never knew.

PRIEST: I require a moment to prepare myself.

WHATTO: An actor, was he? I know so much, I am a compendium of knowledge, yet. And so it always is, the things we do not know are what constitutes our character, **shut up!** (*They are silent. The distant sound of mayhem or carnival. In the stillness,* WHATTO *walks and stops. Some fragments of burned fabric, carried by a wind, blow over the stage, like a cloud of butterflies. He watches them, bewildered.*) I know this stuff. **Time's short.** I know this stuff. **Oh, time's shorter than I thought**! (*Silence, but for* GLORIA'S *brush.* WHATTO *plucks a piece of fabric from the air and examines it.*) Oh ... Oh ... This hung at the window of a drawing-room. I brushed it often on my passage to the lawn. And a child with whom I had acquaintance —

GLORIA: **What sort of acquaintance**. (*Pause*)

WHATTO: Hid in its folds ... (*Pause. He shudders, covering his face with his hands.*)

CHORUS: **Examine your feelings!**

WHATTO: Oh, those autumns of undress and attic rooms ...

CHORUS: **Examine your feelings!**

WHATTO: When we —

CHORUS: **Keep him at bay!**
His sentimental recollections are designed
To drown your
JUDGEMENT!

GLORIA: What ...?

WHATTO (*smiling*): Thought never for a moment of the origins of wealth ...

CHORUS (*outraged*): **You see! Even his confessions are a parody!** (*Pause*)

PRIEST: I'm ready. (WHATTO *looks at him, lost for a moment in reflection.*) Barabbas.

WHATTO (*awakening*): Nor should we have! Even a smile is paid for in some distant place. And raising the tea-cup to your lips, over the rim of which we meet a woman's eyes, **Can't think what slave died for the leaf, can't contemplate the, can you, how ...!** (*The burnt particles pass over.*) High wind. The house is thirty miles away ...

PRIEST: Barabbas. (*Pause. He is about to begin. THE sound of distant carnival or riot.*)

WHATTO: Ssh!

The city has vomited itself ...

The destitute inflamed by lawyers ...

The indigent propelled by journalists ... (*Pause*)

PRIEST: Do you require this or —

WHATTO: Give us Barabbas, do! I also lived in the city. I lay awake and from a vast white bed contemplated the greasy slide of the moon. And the sounds came in my open window. I slept alone. **I slept alone I did, always I slept alone**, three sounds, the bawl of the drunk, the bellow of the woman fucked, the envious scream of the mad. They were, so to speak, in competition, **Nobody say I'm a snob!** And what of Barabbas? (*He looks at* GOODGIRL.) Do you like the moon? I take much comfort from it.

BARABBAS (*to the cross*): They chose me. With one acclaim I don't think there was one dissenting voice they correct me if I'm wrong was there one voice they wanted me if there was one voice I never heard it obviously I articulated their desires you must admit I was the spokesman of the people and you in any case looked a prick your manner was standing there like a china statue designed to cost you whatever little and there wasn't much in any case so. (*Applause and delighted laughter from the assembly which he silences with a gesture.*)

Are you his mum? I feel for you but in some way you must have made him like it did he have no friends and lots of things he said were quite incomprehensible I would have thought a carpenter could find the common touch but look how he this way of so aloof I could have told him that would only and this wandering off all by himself it draws attention to I pitied him but never liked him many people felt that grudging respect which never turned to liking and anyway his criticism made us feel uncomfortable I don't know why I came to crow perhaps but now I can't. (*As if anticipating more applause, the* PRIEST *raises his hand again. Pause.*) **I can do that!** (*He extends his arms like a crucified man.*) **Half a million died like that!** (*He closes his arms tightly round his body, crushing himself.*) I'd like to stay but I've a meeting of the committee of national resistance at half past **Any fool can do that!** (*Pause. At last he relaxes his body. He raises* *his hands in a gesture of dissatisfaction. There is a burst of spontaneous applause.*) It's not what I wanted ... (*He shakes his head.*) No, don't clap it was —

WHATTO: Excellent —

PRIEST: **Not fucking excellent** —

WHATTO: The gifted actor never can be satisfied —

PRIEST: **Not a fucking actor** —

WHATTO: Whatever you say —

PRIEST: Barabbas was greater than that!

WHATTO: Try again later —

PRIEST: **Barabbas was greater and I mocked his genius.** Anybody got my bell? (*He moves with a grudging walk, head down and shaking.*) What is this, anyway? What is it?

WHATTO: I think nothing ill-behoves the performer more than grudging his applause, it's not civil, you break the bond without which all society is —

PRIEST: **I want to break the bonds.** (*Pause.* WHATTO *looks at him, as he mopes among the assembly looking at the floor. This stare continues.*)

AGNEW: I don't think I shall ever be loved.

GOODGIRL: I think that, too!

AGNEW: But at certain times in the development of social forces this lack is diminished, becomes of no significance.

RUBBER: Did anybody bring the sandwiches?

AGNEW: The lack is unfelt in the storm of contrary emotions, for example, justice, even revenge, obliterate this egoistic whine —

GOODGIRL: Egoistic whine?

AGNEW: I call it an egoistic whine —

GOODGIRL: Love? An egoistic whine?

AGNEW: Yes —

FORGET: There are picnic baskets, so there must be sandwiches — (WHATTO *is deep in a conflict, still, yet taut. To* STONEHEART.) Did you bring these?

STONEHEART: I brought a towel. Only a towel.

AGNEW: An egoistic whine, because its whole force is spent in private —

FORGET: Whose basket is this, then?

GOODGIRL: No, that's onanism, surely? That is masturbation you are on about —

AGNEW: All right, that's masturbation, but — (*They are all aware of* WHATTO. *They stare at him. Only the* PRIEST *is still moving among things. And even he stops.*)

WHATTO: I nearly killed. (*He swallows.*) I so nearly killed. (*Pause*) That surely is the limit of absurdity! That is the essence of redundancy when I so soon about to be killed, diced and extirpated even from the memory of my friends, experience **temper. Temper indeed.** (*He gives birth to a laugh.*) No, clearly I am not yet properly prepared. Clearly I still experience a conflict with the world! I am engaged with it — in a spirit of contempt, yes — but engaged — **This repulsive priest who has forsaken all his vows** has — (*Pause. He smiles. He goes to* JANE.) Upset me. (*He shakes his head.*) Absurd.

GLORIA: **And me.**

GOODGIRL (*standing with an inspiration*): There is a further aspect to the Magdalene. I tried to demonstrate her craving for a continuing relation with the body but —

GLORIA: **And me I said.** (*Pause*)

GOODGIRL: All right, I'll do it later. (*Pause*).

GLORIA: I cleaned. (*Pause*)
Someone must. (*Pause*)
And flung the mattresses half-out to air. (*Pause*)
All his visitors. (*Pause*)
Their stains. (*Pause*)
And hair.

RUBBER: I think a sandwich is what I —

GLORIA: Shut up. (*Pause*) Please. **It's a very nice house after all's said and done.** Barren is some ways but. Facing south it gets the sun. **These things please the servants too.** And what a library. What a. Browse, he said. I browsed. I took advantage of his. And some I took back to my room. Under the pillow. **What extraordinary. People do have.** And me the skivvy. My little candle in the march of roofs. **You should have left it at that.** (*Pause.* WHATTO *shrugs, walking slowly.*)

JANE: I don't think anybody cares very much what —

GLORIA: **My testimony** —

JANE: Revelations you are about to —

GLORIA: **My indictment of** —

JANE: Or pities your misfortune —

GLORIA: **The Master.**

JANE: Do we? (*Pause*)

GLORIA: No. Well, you're dead the lot of you. I am among the ghosts.

AGNEW: How true that is! How wholly true and apposite! Though she is a skivvy and illiterate —

FORGET: Not illiterate —

AGNEW: All right, but —

FORGET: Not illiterate, she borrowed books —

AGNEW: Yes, she borrowed books —

FORGET: She said so —

AGNEW: Yes —

FORGET: So how can she —

GLORIA: **Illiterate yes.** (*Pause*) I borrowed them. But they were a sea of shapes to me. A storm of figures where my eyes swam. (*Pause*)

AGNEW: Quote

GLORIA: That's what he liked in me.

AGNEW: Quite.

GLORIA: Ignorance.

AGNEW: Quite.

GLORIA: And poverty.

AGNEW: Quite but illiterate or not you make the pertinent and incon-
testable assertion that at any given moment in the unravelling of
history —

WHATTO: Unravelling?

AGNEW: Of history, a class is dying —

WHATTO: **Unravelling?**

AGNEW: A class is rotting, so it is true to say we live among the
ghosts —

WHATTO: You make it sound like a ribbon —

AGNEW: The ghosts of decaying dispensations —

WHATTO: You make it sound like a wedding —

AGNEW: Perhaps it is a wedding, perhaps —

WHATTO: You make it sound like a bow in a virgin's hair —

AGNEW: If you prefer it, yes, a wedding of new forces whose union
will —

WHATTO (*shuddering with a paroxysm of passion*):
   You
   Make
   Pain
   Eff-
   er-
   vesc-
   ence!

A torrent of cries.

CHORUS: **This is their way**
   Be on your guard!
   Against
   This is their way
   Of sabotaging
   The Millenium!

Silence. Items of burned fabric blow over the stage. WHATTO *reconsti-
tutes himself.* GLORIA, *with immaculate attention, soothes his cheeks
with her hands.*

WHATTO: Lunch was mentioned. Lunch was — (*He removes her
hands as if they were the webs of spiders.*) Clamoured for in varying
degrees —

RUBBER: I'll try a different Joseph —

WHATTO: All the baskets are replete!

GOODGIRL (*to* RUBBER): Didn't you like your Joseph?

RUBBER: I liked it but —

GOODGIRL: I felt the same! I felt whilst Mary was as I portrayed
her, I had neglected other elements!

RUBBER: Joseph had every reason to be bitter, yet —

GOODGIRL: Her spiritual life was so enlarged —

RUBBER: His bitterness would be diluted in some way by —

GOODGIRL: Obviously, and —

RUBBER: Pity, for example, would moderate the —

STONEHEART: I'll try Pilate with less gravity, I think — (*they are passing food among themselves*)

WHATTO: I was afraid of this.

FORGET: I approached Mary from the point of view that she felt anger. First and foremost anger.

AGNEW: Yes, but if I might make a suggestion, this anger would be — I'm not criticizing — transfigured by the knowledge of the power lying behind the sacrifice —

WHATTO: I was afraid of this.

FORGET: Yes —

AGNEW: The confidence that suffering was only — so to speak — a corridor to inexpiable authority!

WHATTO: **I was afraid of this — plethora of interpretation**.

FORGET (*ruminating*): Yes . . .

WHATTO: **This incessant proffering of versions**. It's a madness. It's a fever. By the way, the gates are opened. It really wrecks the soul. Not only open but off their hinges. Why, do you ask? I said to the workmen, one last favour. Giving them each one hundred louis in gold, and a memento of their service, I said remove the gates. These mementos were peculiar and of a highly personal nature, items of underwear or locks of hair which they perhaps deposited in the ditch. Perhaps but not necessarily deposited in the ditch. No, the gates are down in order not to hinder the progress of the mob. Were they merely opened, some panic might inspire me to run the whole length of the drive and in an apotheosis of absurdity attempt to close them on my own. Each weighs a hundred tons. No, it is not my intention to die pinned to my own armorial designs. They are off their hinges, therefore, and flat on the turf. They have fallen. They are eloquent. I should have dismantled the house also but labour is so scarce in times of turmoil. No, we will not proffer more versions. That way lies madness of a different kind to the madness we normally embrace, that way lies **negative madness**. No, put that out of your mind, instead we. (*He stops. They all stop eating. The sandwiches halfway to their mouths. A long howl enters and fills the stage. Dark stains appear on* WHATTO's *clothes. The sound of pattering drops.* JANE *is singing as the howl ceases.*)

JANE: Intolerably innocent
    The judgements of the poor are
    Intolerably simple
    The wild anger of the young
    Intolerably brief
    The satisfaction of our murders
    Intolerably cruel
    Our epitaphs (*She hangs her head, laughing.*)

STONEHEART: You shouldn't have come ... (*She shakes her head.*) How I wanted you to come. But you shouldn't have come. Perhaps there is another life for you. A life of intoxication and shallowness. Certainly the passage of years will alter your view of things. You will ask, how was it I could tolerate the minister of finances? His austerity? His depravity? (*She laughs, shaking her head.*)

WHATTO: She is young enough to have a child. A beautiful child by a husband. This husband will possess more qualities than we at this juncture in our social development can yet anticipate. **Oh, such husbands crowd the horizon! Such wondrous husbands**. Do leave if you wish, the gates are down not only for the rush of the righteous but also to facilitate escape and though your face is subtly coloured by your intimacy with the unforgivable who'd notice in a riot? Those bruises might have come from any where. A dying soldier's boot might just have glanced your cheek.

PRIEST(*entering*): I couldn't find the bell. Instead I found a mirror.

WHATTO: Not difficult.

PRIEST: Not difficult, no. Your walls are —

WHATTO: Thick with them. While my labourers ate turnips I sent to Spain for such —

PRIEST: **He's blood — Your're blood — All blood —**

WHATTO: **All right, it rained.** (*Pause.* WHATTO *takes the mirror from the* PRIEST *and angles it towards the cross, as if to reflect the face of Christ. A shaft of light.* WHATTO *moves, and moves again to direct the mirror.* He moves! He hates the sight! His head goes! And! (*He laughs, angling it again cruelly.*) He shuts his eyes! (*He turns to the* PRIEST.) Why? Why can he not observe himself?

RUBBER: Because he is ashamed ...

WHATTO: Yes ... Yes ...! He *is* ashamed ... (*He thrusts it at the* PRIEST.) Hold it! My arm's aching! (*The* PRIEST *takes the mirror.* WHATTO *stares at the cross, entranced. He shudders with the joy of his discovery. He covers his mouth with his hand. He looks to the others.*) **Look! He is ashamed!** And I know why ...! I know why ...! (*He tears off his coat.*) There were others of Golgotha! Always there are others! (*He tears off his shirt.*) There are those recorded, and those who fail to be recorded, obviously there is **Other testament**! (*He is bare-chested.*) **Always other testament**. (*He bows, smiling, to his friends.*)

GLORIA: And he asked me to his room. To his room, no less. Oh, what a room ... (WHATTO *begins to dance, lifting his knees high and balletic.*) This room I —

WHATTO: There was a lunatic at Golgotha. This lunatic attended crucifixions. It was his passion. And the authorities tolerated it.

BLIND SOLDIER: Whatcha, John ...

WHATTO: And he articulated their — (*Pause. He ceases moving. The sound of mayhem or carnival drifts through.*) Impatience ... (*Pause. He wipes his eyes.* JANE *hurries to him, clutching him.*)

JANE: What are you doing? What are you doing?

GOODGIRL (*jumping to her feet*): Let's run! We can get away! We

can really get away! (*They look at her.*) I haven't lived, have you?
I haven't begun to live and. (*They stare.*) All right. You didn't want
to live. (*She sits clumsily.*)

AGNEW: Your knee is really beautiful. May I kiss it? (*He suddenly
kisses it.*) I did it! And without permission!

WHATTO (*his hands extended like a crucified man*): The testament of
the lunatic at Golgotha. (*The* PRIEST *goes to put down the mirror.*)
Don't put the mirror down. (*Pause*) I beg you. (*Pause*) I beg you all.
To show your customary respect when all the trappings of respect
are. And I in turn will spare you the terrible necessity of dealing
with my corpse. I have attended to everything, as one who intends
to vacate a property should leave it clean.

STONEHEART: You know we love you.

WHATTO: I do know that. And yet. I have thrived on such devotion.
And yet. **He felt at first absurd that I stole His attention**
It's
After All
An
Entertainment
Death
And then to find this. To have to tolerate this. Cavorting and. No,
it spoils the. Naturally he. Within the obvious constraints of.
Expressed his chagrin. (*He emits a long and terrible cry.*) This cry
goes unrecorded in the gospels. (*He repeats it.*) This cry has only
now been excavated. (*And again*) This cry —

CHORUS: **He knows our cries better than anyone!**
He knows the sound of our despair!
The scale of agony he practised daily
And wrung notes from misery of such rare intensity!

LUNATIC: I danced!
I danced!
And few could tear their eyes from me!

*The assembly stands, laughing as an audience laughs at a street performer.
This laughter is orchestrated, rhythmic and consciously flat. During the
laughter,* WHATTO *dances a mockery of* CHRIST *He stops suddenly.
He picks his coat off the floor and slowing buttons it all the way up in
silence.*

LUNATIC: I think his patience hurt me most. Always the patient ones.
The bearers. The demonstrators of fortitude. They drove me to an
excess of invention. (*Pause. The assembly are rigid all this time.*) And
in the night he engaged me in a conversation. This conversation goes
unrecorded in the gospels. This conversation has only now been
unearthed.

RUBBER: You are insane. I'll cure you. (*Pause.* WHATTO *pretends
to think.*)

LUNATIC: The blind soldier you —

CHRIST: Never mind him.

LUNATIC: He also had a disability —

CHRIST: Never mind him. (*Pause*) Do you want to be cured? I have strength for one more miracle. (*Pause*)

LUNATIC: I don't know. (*Pause*) I don't know, you see — (*He laughs.*) I don't know if I'm not **vastly happier like this**.

CHRIST: Touch me.

LUNATIC: No, I don't think I —

CHRIST: My foot, just —

LUNATIC (*childishly*): No! Absolutely not! (*Pause*) Anyway, it's all — **Why do you want me to be sane?** What's in it for you? (*Pause*)

CHRIST: I have had the most terrible life in the world. Please pity me . . .

LUNATIC: No.

CHRIST: I have been a purpose and not a person. Do pity me . . .

LUNATIC: No!

CHRIST: I lived without intimacy and yet I was not without feelings.

LUNATIC: **No pity no.** How could I do this job if I was. How could I.

CHRIST: They had free will. I alone had no free will. **Yet I had feelings**.

LUNATIC: You think it's easy being here? **All the time I'm here. In all weathers and you say**. No, pity's for those with.

CHRIST: Was ever a man less free than me? (*Pause.* WHATTO *goes to the cross and runs his hands over it, reaching slowing and vainly for the feet of* CHRIST.)

BLIND SOLDIER: Whatcha doing, John?

LUNATIC: Oh, nothing, just.

BLIND SOLDIER: All right, then.

LUNATIC: Merely.

BLIND SOLDIER: All right, then. (*Pause.* WHATTO *goes to touch the cross again when* AGNEW *speaks.*)

AGNEW: There are conditions under which a certain personality exists. With the removal of those conditions, the personality disintegrates. He who was in one condition awesome, lethal or intransigent becomes in the other eccentric, pitiful, absurd. (*He shudders, with laughter or tears.*) I so liked your company, I did thrive on his company . . .! (*He stops.*) And this decay we cannot arrest. It is the very opposite of dentistry, from which I now **wholly disassociate myself**. (*He shudders again.*) I filled his jaw! I polished him! (*He stops. He gets up.*) You see, they are getting very close and we must choose. Certainly I now regard dentistry as a **Reactionary Practice**. (*To* GOODGIRL) No, don't touch me I am excellent. That gesture is full of kindness but the kindness of a superior disdain, I am excellent, thank you, and not at all in need of. Absolutely not but we must choose because refusing choice is choosing also **This man is the product of a dead culture** which sadly we cannot ignore, which sadly cannot be left among the undergrowth like a fallen urn and we must stop laughing at his antics, stand up those who believe in the future. (*No one moves.*) I

said stand up all. (*He laughs.*) You see, it requires tremendous courage
to. In some conditions even cross the street but we. (WHATTO *goes
to him and wraps him in his arms.* AGNEW *weeps pitifully.* FORGET
sings.)

FORGET: I did not marry for love
ALL: **What a relief that is**
   What a futile ambition
FORGET: I did not have children
ALL: **What a false hope that it**
   What a miscalculation
FORGET: I buried my husband
ALL: **He gave you no trouble**
   At least he ignored you
FORGET: And slept with my servant
ALL: **Do you think that will save you**?

*The distant sound of carnival or mayhem. They follow it in unison with
their heads tilted.*)

GOODGIRL: When we are dead there will be such a flood of pity!
Won't there? And this pity will render a correct estimation of our
guilt impossible. We shall be obliterated. My beauty for example,
and the circumstances of my death, together will create so powerful
an image in the mind of subsequent generations I. (*She wrings her
hands. Pause.*) I mean if you wait for the judgement of history you
could. Because just when the truth was creeping from its chrysalis,
trembling, damp, some swooping thing could. Out the sky some. And
darkness again. Some new system dutifully pulping the old. (*She wrings
and wrings.*) I so want to be judged properly but when. **It might not
ever**.
GLORIA: I'll wash it down.
GOODGIRL: Will you . . .
GLORIA: Whatever
      Sluice it.
      Mop and sunshine.
GOODGIRL: Yes . . .
GLORIA: It is the pleasure of my job.
GOODGIRL: Is it . . .
GLORIA: **I also am history**.
GOODGIRL: Well, yes . . . Yes, you are . . . (*A Pause*)
WHATTO: Thank God for my Great Art. (*A wind. They all exhale
deeply.* WHATTO'*s shoulders appear to be shaking with suppressed
laughter. They all inhale deeply. At last the* PRIEST *drops the mirror,
which breaks.*) What's revolution but the rehabilitation of the police?
(*Pause*)
   The interrogator? (*Pause*)
   And the
   Don't say it

Don't say it
All right I won't
   Say it (*He waits. They inhale together, looking each other in the eyes, profoundly.*)
This part was never the worst! I found it on the contrary not without its comedy, not without its irony and they, even they, saw this, they even, understood these aspects and as a consequence, the best of them broke with fear, they threw fear aside because it humiliated them! (*Pause*) They waded through fear. And I admired it. I saw the very best of man. (*Pause*) But we are friends which makes it so much more. (*Pause.* STONEHEART *makes a single move to break the stillness.*)

JANE: You would ... ! Of all people, you would ...! And how you claimed corruption! How you confessed the rotten condition of your soul! (*He looks at her.*) But obviously, this claim was a drapery on such **Magnificence**. (*Pause*) The water-colours, who will inherit these, or is inheritance, of course it is, a relic of our declining order, shall I or (*she closes her eyes.*) Don't touch me again, will you, since every touch was. (*Pause*) I don't think we used the word love, did we? As a verb? And won't now, obviously. (STONEHEART *covers his face with his hands. He struggles to master himself.* WHATTO *goes to him and taking him with infinite solicitude, draws him towards the cross. The assembly inhales in unison.*)

WHATTO: The first thing is not to change the subject, which is the habit of a dentist, the habit of a child's physician. On the contrary I found with minds as fine as yours only the subject itself would do, there is a dignity in that unblinking concentration on death which. Can you say death?

STONEHEART: I can say death.

WHATTO: Which honours everyone, myself included, and if the first is willing, how much easier the path becomes for those of feebler dispositions, **if feebleness it is I don't judge**. (*He leads* STONEHEART *into a position for execution against the upright of the cross, and helps him kneel.*) The world is coming apart or as I prefer to put it, we no longer fit. (*He shakes out a cord.*) This is the cord. I never conceal the cord, on the contrary I — (*He stops. He almost chokes.*)

My
Friend
My
Dear
My

WHATTO *lets out a cry and simultaneously strangles* STONEHEART. *The thing done, he rocks on his knees, to and fro, for an inordinate length of time in silence.*

GOODGIRL: Jane obviously has the right to
         But I
         Jane must follow if she wants but (*A pause.* GLORIA

drops the bucket with a clatter. Water pours over the floor. She stands fixed with disbelief.) That's gone over my dress . . .

WHATTO: I have no preferences but obviously a certain rhythm makes for —

GOODGIRL: My silly dress is all —

WHATTO: Comforts in some way the fluctuating nerves which —

GOODGIRL: I did not think the dress was silly until she spoiled it and now —

WHATTO: We experience on such occasions —

GOODGIRL: **Why is that**? (*She lifts the wet hem.*) It seems already like a thing from a museum . . .

WHATTO: **I mean go if you want to.** (*Pause*)

AGNEW: It's funny but
       Excuse by baseness but
       It hurts I daresay?
       This is utterly base and I call myself an intellectual!
       But it must hurt and. (*Pause. He stands, adjusting himself.*) No one quarrels with my right to — (*He looks around him.*) Of course, going through a door will not be painless, I know that, how shall I, would you like me to —

WHATTO: Shh . . .

AGNEW: Sit or —

WHATTO: Shh . . . (WHATTO *draws him to the cross.*)

AGNEW: I can't stop talking, do forgive me, the minister said very little but I don't have his dignity, do, my volubility is. (*Feeling the cord he stops.*)

WHATTO: How rare it is to die at the hand of a friend . . .

AGNEW: Yes . . .

WHATTO: An impatience to be gone . . . .

AGNEW: Yes . . . and it is not as if I were a believer . . .

WHATTO: No! Not at all! No rewards!

AGNEW: No rewards, no, but rather the — (*He is stopped by the cord. As soon as* AGNEW *dies* RUBBER *jumps to his feet.*)

RUBBER: I want to play the executioner!

WHATTO: I don't think —

RUBBER: The executioner, yes!

WHATTO: I don't think there is time, quite frankly —

RUBBER: **The testament of him who drove the nails in**!

WHATTO: I hate to spoil an inspiration but I can't avoid the suspicion you are prevaricating, which is unnecessary, after all, the gates are down, and —

RUBBER: **I'm not afraid I'm inspired**. (WHATTO *shrugs.*)

WHATTO: Yes. Yes. Go ahead. I was being mechanical. I was seduced by my own rhythm. I allowed my own aesthetic to. Act. Act away by all means.

GLORIA: **I'm fetching the police**. (*They stare at her.*) Not police. There are no police the people. (*Their stares are full of ridicule.*) Them. I mean. Them. (*She waves a hand towards the mayhem. Her hand falters.*)

WHATTO: But they want us dead. As you do ... (*Pause*)

GLORIA: All right, they do. But ... (WHATTO *smiles*.) They want to do it themselves.

WHATTO: **True**

> **True**
>
> **True** (*They laugh in staccato rhythms.*)
>
> **True**
>
> **True**
>
> **True** (*They laugh again.*)
>
> How they hate to be deprived
>
> How they hate to lose the satisfaction of the
>
> **Unadulterated pleasure of revenge**
>
> Which I for all my history have never known
>
> Not once
>
> It was my career the solitary practice of an expertise ... (*Pause*)

RUBBER: I begin!

WHATTO (*awaking*): And I listen!

EXECUTIONER: **Jesus of Nazareth!** (*Pause*) **Jesus of Nazareth!**

WHATTO: Oh, is that me?

> I hardly
>
> Surely
>
> Someone must be
>
> Oh, all right! (*He grins.*)
>
> Since you press me!

EXECUTIONER: **I have come to drive these through your hands and knees**

PRIEST: Feet ...

EXECUTIONER (*turning cruelly on the* PRIEST): For years I've heard your version. For years. Know All. And I say it was knees. (*The* PRIEST *shrugs. He turns back to the cross.*) Be good. For struggling's pointless.

WHATTO: My own words exactly. (*Pause*)

EXECUTIONER: But he did. (*Everyone groans.*) This isn't known! This was not previously recorded! (*They hiss.*) You see, you hate the truth! You drown the facts in sentiment! I could not write or I should have made notes! (*They protest.*) He was too great to suffer silently! **He found life wonderful!** (*He affirms with nods of his head, over their racket.*) He found it wonderful because —

WHATTO: **Shhh!** (*They stop.*)

EXECUTIONER: Unlike us, everything was going his way ... (*Pause. He walks to the cross and puts himself in the position for death.* WHATTO *goes to him, and takes out the silk rope. The assembly inhale in unison.* RUBBER *dies with a toss of his head. The* PRIEST *takes off his biretta, holds it loosely a moment, and then allows it to fall to the floor.*)

PRIEST: No one said

> As yet and I presume nobody will

Beg my services therefore

And in any case I was insincere being affected with all manner of revolutionary sentiments a peculiar and intangible faith both rational and mystical a real cocktail of half-digested and (*Pause*)

I was badly paid and this can

Oh, that is a terrible erosion of belief, the pay!

WHATTO: Do stop confessing ...

PRIEST: Was I? Was I confessing?

WHATTO: I think so, yes ...

PRIEST: To whom, I wonder? (*He points.*) He's in the way ... (*He indicates the body of* RUBBER *lying over* AGNEW. WHATTO *shrugs.*) So what? When we consider the. (*The sound of rioting carried by the wind.*) It will be the normal **I refuse** practice of all I **refuse**! (*He tears offstage. Pause.* WHATTO *looks after him.*)

WHATTO: His congregation certainly was dwindling. Did you attend much at the end? I never did.

GOODGIRL: He wanted happiness. A thing I learned at such a young age to put out of mind. The freedom you acquire the moment you. I'll go. (WHATTO *smiles.*) And people said my neck was the best thing ...! (*She laughs.*) I'll sit here, shall I? (*She goes to the cross.*) Already I feel the merest fragment of a history! I look down on the passage of my time! Do you need to damage the neck, it seems a pity?

WHATTO: There is a bruise but.

GOODGIRL: A bruise can be.

WHATTO: It can.

GOODGIRL: Not attractive exactly but.

WHATTO: A fascination all the same. A signature to some forever secret deed. Sit there. Didn't we enjoy the summers? And this is a summer of precisely the same character as those —

GOODGIRL: You are patronizing me. (*He stops, with horror*)

WHATTO: Was I?

GOODGIRL: Yes.

WHATTO (*disturbed*): Was I ...

GOODGIRL: With none of the others did you attempt to divert attention from your task. You talked of death. The thing itself was not disguised, but with me you ...! **I could be so angry ...!** (*She closes her eyes.*)

WHATTO: Forgive me.

GOODGIRL (*shakes her head*): No, that's unforgivable ...! (*She shakes her head again.*) Even at ... Here even ... (WHATTO *kills her swiftly, releases the cord and runs insanely round the stage, tearing at his clothes and tossing his wig to the floor.*)

CHORUS: **Imperfect**
   Imperfect
   The gift has gone
   IMPERFECT RESOLUTION of a life!

How
It
Offends
His
Practice

WHATTO *stops, clutching his wrists in despair. As he stands fixedly, white paper, smouldered, blows across the stage like butterflies in flocks. He relaxes.* GLORIA *laughs out loud.*

GLORIA: The library! The library! (*She puts out her hands to catch pieces.*)

JANE (*who has remained staring at the body of* STONEHEART): It is in the absences that great love knows itself. Not in the embrace.

WHATTO: Yes ... (*Pause*) I say yes ... I ... (GLORIA *laughs as she chases the burned books.*) I ... (*He extends the cord.*) Imagine ...

JANE: No.

WHATTO: No? Are you pretending that you have a future?

JANE: Yes.

WHATTO: After him? A future? After **him**?

JANE: A difference.

WHATTO: Yes, but —

JANE: A difference, that's all, not a —

WHATTO: **He shaped your soul**. (*Pause. He extends the cord again.*) Come on, be realistic. (*He shudders.*) I don't persuade you! I don't exhort you! **Whatto him who wept most days** no I don't persuade you the gates are down and they are in the gardens listen the music of the future the falling urns and the fouling of the fountains this is the perfect climate for a woman of your temperament **whose every thought was complicated by reflection and by sensuality** yes this is a world in which you'll flourish **that skirt cost seven hundred louis**. (*He stares at her, smiling. She engages his eyes infinitely. Suddenly he lurches at her. She dodges him, breathlessly. For the second time she unbuttons herself. In her shift, she stands in the ruins of her fallen couture.*)

JANE: Some chance in this. (WHATTO *shakes his head.*) Some anonymity in this. (*He shakes it again.*)

WHATTO: The brain. The brain will betray you ...

JANE: **That also can be stripped**. (*They stare. Suddenly she seizes* WHATTO *in her arms and hugs him. Then she flees. He remains still, the cord limp in his hands.* GLORIA *is skipping around laying burned pages on the floor. She looks up at him.*)

GLORIA: Ours, now.

WHATTO: Yes ...

GLORIA: Ours, now, the library ...

WHATTO: Yes ... (*He looks at* FORGET, *seated on the ground.*) You try to tell them ...! But they know best! You give them the benefit of how many years? But they know best!

FORGET: Who's killing you? (*He smiles.*)

WHATTO: I thought no one would ever ask! I thought — all this equality in the air — I thought — that's the first thing they'll want to know! (FORGET *climbs to her feet*.)

FORGET: I thought of going down the garden and dancing. They like to dance, don't they? I thought, seeing me dance, they'll let their anger slip ...

WHATTO: Which dance? (*His face is full of bemused pity*.) Your dance? But that's a dance of privilege ...! **Even the dancing is coloured**. (*She shrugs. He takes her kindly by the arm*.) Oh, we wish to slip through! We wish to crawl by! We long to be worms but all over us there hangs the odour of our lives, there hangs the terrible miasma of our choices ... (FORGET *draws her hood over her face*. WHATTO *despatches her swiftly*.)

GLORIA: (*on her hands and knees with scraps of paper*): Now, this one I read! (*She looks up*.) I call it reading. This one I recognize!

WHATTO: Tell them I'm here.
       The Seigneur.
       The Executioner of Despotic will.
       Awaits their just revenge.
       Say that.

GLORIA (*as* WHATTO *turns to adjust his necktie*): I could have but you touched me. I could have carried your last orders but. It ended service your appalling kiss. **You think love's a bathtub?** (*He finishes his tie*.) **You think my body was for rinsing in?**

WHATTO: Pick up my wig. (*She shakes her head*.) Absurd object a wig I feel sure there will be legislation to put paid to wigs, the new man after all must be — (*He picks it up himself. Beats it on his leg*.) Unlike the old. (*He puts it on*.) Hold the mirror. (*She shakes her head*.) All right, a shard of glass.

GLORIA: **Love's not a shoe**.

WHATTO: No? It pinches, evidently ... (*He bends. He picks up a sliver of mirror. He looks in it, plucks his wig. She stares at him, he places his back to her*.) Not a shoe? What is it, then? (*Pause. She heaves with resentment*.) Your body smelled ... (*He plucks his wig*.)
    If I remember, of ... Labour ... Devotion ... And ... Neglect ... (*some shouts and damage nearer than before*) I thought ... Was it dark or light? Was it the afternoon? I forget ... I thought.. she smells of ... self-contempt ... her sweat ... is the sweat of the never-loved ...

WHATTO (*stands with his hands by his sides, prepared.* GLORIA *grabs up the cord* WHATTO *left ostentatiously in her reach and throws it over* WHATTO'*s neck. He lets out a triumphant cry, but* GLORIA'*s expertise is not great. He staggers with her, and in the peculiar silence of their dance, a* CHILD *appears, wearing the* PRIEST'*s biretta and* JANE'*s shift on top of his/her own garments. He/she watches this absurd spectacle until catching his/her eye,* GLORIA *ceases her efforts*.

WHATTO: No ... ! No ... ! (*He holds his hurt neck.*) Finish it ...!
(*He also sees the* CHILD. *The sounds of destruction and laughter float
on the air. A pause, of deep examination.*) How badly she was doing
it. You try. (*The* CHILD *merely looks.*) How incredibly incompetent,
which only indicates the incompatibility of passion and efficiency.
I was cold. Always. (*Pause. The* CHILD *stares at him.*) You try.
(*Pause*) Which is not to corrupt you! Heaven knows! (*The* CHILD
goes to WHATTO *and taking his hand, puts it to his lips.*)

CHILD: Long live Gentlemen! (*Pause. He looks into* WHATTO's *eyes
and takes his hands again.*) Long live Gentlemen! (WHATTO *Stares
into his eyes.*)

WHATTO: There is no such thing ... (*The* CHILD *falls into* WHATTO's
arms, sobbing. WHATTO *rocks him, soothingly. The sound of the crowd
grows louder.* GLORIA *sings, to a single drum.*)

GLORIA: God give us the courage of our cruelty
     God
     God
     give the power to hurt
     God
     God rip out my sympathy and the thing I call the woman
       in me! (*The light shrivels to the face of* WHATTO.)
     Or (*Tap*)
     We

Tap. The light goes out. In the darkness a massive exhalation of breath.